The Faith That

PHOENIX FIRST ASSEMBLY
13613 N. Cave Creek Rd.
Phoenix, AZ 85022

Library
Oakland S.U.M.

HARPER JUBILEE BOOKS

239
ORR

958

The Faith That Persuades

PHOENIX FIRST ASSEMBLY
13613 N. Cave Creek Rd.
Phoenix, AZ. 85022

J. Edwin Orr
D. Phil. (Oxford)
Ed. D. (California)

A HARPER JUBILEE BOOK

HARPER & ROW, PUBLISHERS
New York, Hagerstown, San Francisco, London

THE FAITH THAT PERSUADES. Copyright © 1977 by J. Edwin Orr.
All rights reserved. Printed in the United States of America. No
part of this book may be used or reproduced in any manner
whatsoever without written permission except in the case of
brief quotations embodied in critical articles and reviews. For
information address Harper & Row, Publishers, Inc., 10 East
53rd Street, New York, N.Y. 10022. Published simultaneously in
Canada by Fitzhenry & Whiteside Limited, Toronto.

A HARPER JUBILEE BOOK ORIGINAL

FIRST EDITION
Designed by Stephanie Krasnow

Library of Congress Cataloging in Publication Data

Orr, James Edwin, 1912–
  The faith that persuades.
  (A Harper jubilee book original; HJ 30)
  Bibliography: p.
  1. Apologetics—20th century. 2. Religion and science—
1946– 3. Religion—Philosophy. I. Title.
BT1102.O77   239   76–62924
ISBN 0–06–066939–X

77 78 79 80 10 9 8 7 6 5 4 3 2 1

*Gratitude is expressed
to Mr. Thomas F. Staley,
for his encouragement of
apologetics evangelism*

Contents

The Faith That Persuades

GEORGE de WOLFE
8613 E BERRIDGE LANE
SCOTTSDALE ARIZONA 85253

CHAPTER ONE

Science and the Fallacies

A teacher in Santa Monica decided to write on the subject of alcoholism for his Ph.D. dissertation at UCLA. He knew that this was more demanding than writing a term paper for high school. To earn a doctorate in philosophy in any field, one must make a contribution to the field of knowledge. In this regard, he had a serious problem. "What new thing could I discover about alcoholism," he thought, "when people have been getting drunk for many thousands of years?"

He wrestled with the problem and came up with a possible answer. He took it to his mentor for consideration.

"If," said he, "I could discover the common denominator in cases of drunkenness, perhaps I could discover the cause of alcoholism?"

"Good idea!" replied the professor. "Work on it."

But the fact that he himself was a total abstainer posed a further problem. Then he remembered an old fellow on skid row, an intermittent drunkard, who offered to do all of the research for him for nothing but the raw materials.

The reports came rolling in from the enterprising wino. On Monday, he got drunk with whiskey and soda; and on Tuesday, he got drunk with brandy and soda; on Wednesday, he got drunk with rum and soda; but on Thursday, he got drunk with gin and soda; while on Friday, he got drunk with vodka and soda. And so it went.

Johnson had a mathematical mind. He asked himself: "So what makes him get drunk? It must be the common denominator. It must be the soda!"

That illustrates facetiously the foolishness of fallacies. Conclusions can be drawn from a common denominator, but other factors cannot be ignored. Alcohol, not soda, is the cause of drunkenness.

And so it is with certain of the fallacies citing scientists against the faith. Simply stated, they sound convincing; but they are utterly fallacious, and principles involved demand a thorough reexamination.

Irkutsk in winter is a drab but busy metropolis far east of Moscow in the Asian part of the USSR. It is not far south of the latitude of Verhoyansk, the coldest of all inhabited places in the world, so its winter is chillingly cold. I was glad not to have to spend too much time on the streets, but entertained myself inspecting the university.

Having concentrated in geography-geology for the first postgraduate degree, I was interested in seeing Siberia's fascinating Lake Baikal nearby, a lake as large as all of Switzerland, and a mile deep.

Sacha Sergeivitch Samarin, a university language student with an unlikely trace of an Oxford accent, was appointed to take a party of us to Baikal,[1] so heavily iced that our jovial chauffeur drove the car onto the ice. I decided to engage Sacha Sergeivitch in conversation, hoping to direct the talk into channels spiritual rather than material.

Before long, the amiable young Russian and I were talking about matters scientific, so I interjected a provocative observation about science and faith. Sacha, like every other good Intourist guide, had been told not to tangle with the tourists on matters of religion—some such visitors were handicapped by old-fashioned notions in education, and too cutting a remark was likely to hurt their feelings. But with a tourist both educated and friendly, Sacha felt that he was able to communicate.

Science Disproves

"But," said he, "does anyone with a scientific education believe in God nowadays?"

"Do you have a scientific education?" I asked.

"No," he replied. "But I have studied some science. My interest lies in literature, but I have enjoyed certain science courses."

"Me, too," I assured him. "I have been interested in the sciences all my life. But," I went on, "I was not aware of any scientific arguments against the idea of God."

Sacha was astounded.

"Are you serious?" he inquired.

"Certainly."

We trudged through the snow, somewhat removed from the other tourists and the chauffeur accompanying them. I reopened the conversation:

"Sacha, would you agree that during the past seventy-odd years, scientists have discovered hundreds of thousands of facts?"

He thought it over, interested in spite of himself, but looking for a possible trap in the innocent question.

"Could you name one such fact so discovered that contradicts the idea of God?"

Sacha did not answer. I teased him with a few facetious suggestions, and he seriously ruled them out. By default, he conceded that scientists had not discovered a single fact that contradicted the idea of God.

"All right," I went on. "Would you agree that during the past seventy-odd years, scientists have propounded thousands of theories to explain these facts?"

Sacha readily agreed. I pointed out that some of these theories have been discarded, such as the notion that radio waves were transmitted through ether; and some were in suspense, for lack of evidence; but many had been adopted as working hypotheses.

"Would you agree, Sacha, that the Russian space projects and the American space projects are based upon the same scientific theories?"

He agreed.

"Very well, then," I proceeded. "Could you name a single scientific theory that contradicts the idea of God?"

Sacha kicked the snow from his tracks as he further gave thought to the question. To tease him, I suggested:

"How about the theory of gravitation? Does that theory contradict the idea of God? If so, how do you explain the fact that Sir Isaac Newton, who propounded the theory, himself believed in God?"

Sacha was quick to protest.

"But, sir, that was three hundred years ago, when everyone believed in God. It was the fashion then."

"Very well," I answered. "Let's consider the twentieth century. Many people regard Professor Albert Einstein as the greatest scientist of the twentieth century. He propounded the theory of relativity. He suggested all sorts of tests for its validity, and it is generally accepted today. Does that theory contradict the idea of God? If so, how do you explain the fact that Albert

Einstein professed to believe in God in his way?"

Again, Sacha did not answer. I was ready to hear him suggest, as a young American had suggested, that the "steady-state cosmology"—the idea that the universe is eternal and self-sustaining—nullified the idea of God; and I was equally eager to quote the latest scientific opinion that "this very interesting speculation to date had produced no observable evidence." But Sacha remained silent, suggesting that the Soviet scientists were more committed to the "big-bang" theory of the expanding universe. Finally, Sacha ventured:

"Does not the theory of evolution contradict the idea of God?"

"Without committing myself one way or the other," I said, carefully, "I must point out to you that there is not a single development propounded by the theorists of evolution that could not be explained by saying 'That's the way that God accomplished His creation.'"

While Sacha was digesting the argument, I explained to him that there was a standard text on the elements of biology in use throughout the secular universities of the United States, in which Prof. Paul B. Weisz declared that the idea of evolution is not any more or any less antireligious than the idea of special creation, for neither really strengthens, weakens or otherwise affects belief in God. "To the religious person, only the way God operates, not God as such, is in question."[2]

Sacha Sergeivitch Samarin gave an uncomfortable laugh. He repeated an oft-told tale.

"When our pioneer cosmonauts returned from orbiting the earth," he recalled, "one of them said that they had looked so carefully for God up there and they did not see him anywhere! This shocked some of our older believers."

"But not any educated believers," I protested. "I am very surprised that any educated Russian, cosmonaut or other, should even consider looking for God in orbit around the earth. What kind of a God do they think that Christians other than infants believe in?"

"At our university," explained Sacha, "we were told that in the English-speaking world the scientists had discarded the old ideas of God, and that only old-fashioned believers still held to the notion. Is not this so?"

"In Europe and America," I rejoined, "there are scientists who believe and scientists who do not believe, scientists who say they know and scientists who are agnostic. Science is neutral when it comes to religious faith, but that does not mean that scientists are always or even often neutral. One of our greatest scientists was the late Arthur H. Compton. A couple of pages in the encyclopedia are devoted to his discoveries. Let me quote to you what he declared: 'Science is the glimpse of God's purpose in nature. The very existence of the amazing world of the atom and radiation points to a purposeful creation, to the idea that there is a God and an intelligent purpose back of everything.' "[3]

In Irkutsk, I tried to locate the Evangelical congregation, but was informed by my guides that no such church existed. One cold morning, at breakfast, a Russian unwittingly sat down at my table and, when he discovered that I had served in the United States Air Force in World War II, he was enthusiastic. He assured me that there was a Baptist house—as he called it—less than a kilometer away. So I told my Intourist guide that he need no longer help me find the Baptist house; that a Red Army veteran had told me where to find it. The device worked. He hurried away, returning shortly to say that his colleagues had just discovered the location of the church, and that he would take me. But the pastor was suspicious of a visitor thus introduced by an obvious atheist until I told him that my profession was that of Philip's, which convinced him but fooled our listener.

Science Invalidates

Tashkent, the metropolis of Soviet Central Asia, proved to be a very interesting city, destined—sad to say—to be wrecked by an earthquake shortly after my visit. I stayed at an Intourist hotel, and spent the time walking the streets and studying the polyglot population, among whom the Uzbek people predominated.

Soviet educators had greatly reduced illiteracy in these Central Asia republics, and not a few Uzbek professional people spoke a passable English as well as fluent Russian. I found an Uzbek schoolteacher, whose face reminded me of friends in China, cautiously willing to carry on a conversation. We began by discussing Uzbek culture. Finally, I told her about my conversation with a university student (unnamed, for obvious reasons) in Irkutsk. Mme Khoja, as one may call her, obviously had a Muslim background, but had studied in Tashkent in Russian and in Samarkand in Uzbek. She made a very perceptive observation:

"Sir, I am not so foolish as to say that science contradicts the idea of God; but science explains everything, and that makes the idea of God superfluous, irrelevant. I do not need God or Allah, thanks to science."

"Science explains everything?" I asked, raising eyebrows.

"Very well," she retorted. "I shall qualify that by saying that science is on its way to explaining everything."

"Science," I suggested gently, "explains many things that uneducated people had attributed directly to God. When I was a little boy of four, I heard the thunder roll, and I told my mother that God was moving his furniture upstairs.

"But, does science explain anything? Come into my kitchen and ask me, 'Why is the kettle boiling?' I reply, 'The kettle is boiling because the combustion of the gas transfers heat to the bottom of the kettle which, being a good conductor, transfers it immediately to the water. The molecules of water become agitated; they spin around and make a singing noise, and finally give off water in the form of steam; and that is why the kettle is boiling.'

"Then my wife comes into the kitchen, and you ask her, 'Why is the kettle boiling?' And she tells you: 'The kettle is boiling because I am going to make you some tea.' "

Mme Khoja laughed heartily.

"I did not tell you why the kettle was boiling," I added. "I told you how the kettle is boiling. And science does not tell us the why of anything, really, but only the how and what."

"I understand your point," said the Uzbek lady, "but I am sure there must be an answer to it."

"Look at it this way," I told her. "Liquids commonly contract when they freeze. The great exception is water which expands into ice. Ask a physicist why this is so, and he will tell you that he cannot explain why, but that he knows that this is how water behaves. I would say that the reason that water expands upon freezing is that otherwise the seas and lakes and rivers would freeze from the bottom up, and make life impossible on this planet. Have you a better philosophy?"

One of the American astronauts, not one of those who proclaimed a Christian faith, commending something that I written, took exception to a statement of mine that, just as a poor old washerwoman with the blessing of eyesight knows more about the beauty of the spectrum than the most brilliant mathematician born blind who could measure the wave length of light, so likewise a poor old washerwoman with the blessing of faith knows more about the why of the universe than a brilliant unbeliever. He contended that this was contemptuous of the great discoveries of scientists. Quite the contrary. Readily conceded are all the triumphs of scientific achievement, with the proviso that none of them explain the "why" of things, only the "how" and the "what."

Science Dismisses

It took an English-speaking visitor to the Soviet Union to propound the third popular pseudoscientific fallacy. In a Moscow hotel, with a Russian Baptist pastor present, Prof. Reader Michaelson unexpectedly sided with his atheist host against the two believers at table.

"I would concede immediately," he asserted, "that our friend Orr is eminently correct in saying that science does not disprove the existence of God. This is exactly so. But it must be added that neither does science prove the existence of God. In fact, on this important subject, science offers no evidence whatsoever. Therefore, in the total absence of evidence, why should anyone wish to believe in such an unsupported and unsupportable proposition."

The eminent professor's fallacy surely lay in the naive assumption that the only evidence to be considered had to be scientific evidence. But it is obvious that there are other kinds of evidence than scientific evidence. There is also legal evidence, and historical evidence, and other sorts not readily demonstrated in a laboratory.

"In Long Beach, a city in Southern California," I explained to my Russian friends, "a certain lawyer was charged with the murder of his wife and her lover. His alibi presented in court affirmed that, on the night of the murder, he was in Las Vegas, in Nevada, hundreds of miles away, at the notorious gambling tables.

"He was unable to sustain his alibi," I went on, "so he was sentenced to life in prison. Now, what did he need to gain an acquittal? Just two witnesses. Did they need to be scientists? No, school dropouts would have sufficed. If he had produced a taxi-driver and a waitress, and if the taxi-driver had asserted that he met the man at the airport at eight in the evening, and if the waitress had affirmed that she had served the fellow a cup of coffee at ten, he would have gone free.

"Of course, the taxi-driver and the waitress would have been subjected to cross-examination by the prosecution to confirm or discredit their stories. They could not have contradicted each other. Legal experts have their own recognized way, as systematic as scientists in a laboratory, of assessing the evidence. I would say that basically the Christian faith is based upon the testimony of witnesses, that the reason why the Christian religion spread so rapidly throughout the Roman Empire was that there were more than four hundred eyewitnesses still alive a quarter of a century afterwards to testify that they had seen Jesus Christ alive from the dead."

"Maybe some believed that then," said Michaelson, "but that was a long time ago."

"There is such a thing as historical evidence," I added. "And there is a historical method for assessing it, just as there is a scientific method. George Washington crossed the Delaware River to take the Hessian garrison at Trenton by surprise. They were expecting Santa Claus, not George. There is no scientific evidence for this event. A team of geologists on the banks of the Delaware would find no mark of evidence in the rocks around. But there is plenty of historical evidence—the diary of Washington, the records of the Continental and the British armies.

"And it can be said that the narrative of the Gospels is better attested today by historians than ever before. The statements it makes that can be cross-checked have been proved to be true. It has the ring of truth."

The Ring of Truth

One snowy Saturday, I hailed a taxi and gave the driver the address of the Moscow Baptist Church, but was refused. I decided to seek out the place alone, and began the journey. On the Moscow Underground, descending an escalator, I sought the help of a younger man who, unaware that it was the address of a church, kindly changed his direction and accompanied me by various routes until we emerged in the snow and took our places in a line awaiting a trolley bus. In German, he told me that the waiting passengers were certain that the bus line needed was 11A, but that no one knew which stop.

A darker-skinned man approached and said in English:

"May I be of service?"

"Thank you. You are from India?"

"Indian Embassy. You know our country?"

"I have visited sixteen states."

He shook hands cordially, took over direction from the kindly engineer, and boarded a bus with me, also uncertain of the proper stop. We were both standing, strap-hanging, my back to the driver, when suddenly I noticed a middle-aged lady hooded in a babushka, whose face reclined in such repose that I could not help but think, "You are a Christian." As if she read my thoughts, she replied with a smile, "Da," and a tentative contact was made.

Assuring my Indian friend that I had found the way to the church, I followed the lady off the bus, and was joined by a group in animated conversation, all on their way to the church. Meeting? Saturday night? Pastor Michael Zhidkov explained that it was a midweek service formerly held on Wednesday evenings, but crowded out, and now arranged for Tuesday, Thursday, and Saturday. The auditorium was overcrowded, the choir sang ten times, there was ardent intercession, there were four sermons of biblical content, and the whole service lasted two and a half hours.

Despite Indoctrination

In Kiev, the rebuilt capital of the Ukraine, I persuaded an Intourist girl to call me a taxi to take me to the Intourist office before closing time, to collect long-lost mail. Within a day, I was questioned by a plainclothes investigator as to why I had not used the airport bus.

Officials informed me that there was no Evangelical church in Kiev, but relented after subtle persuasion and took me to the nearest congregation. Five hundred people crowded a hall with three hundred seats. Again, the choir sang ten times, there were four sermons, simultaneous audible prayer was offered, and even more fervent was the meeting. I was placed on the platform behind the pastors, and introduced to the congregation.

Tanya Kirichenka came from the university to provide me with tourist assistance. She was a bright girl, puzzled to find a visiting graduate an obvious believer. She finally confided: "I prayed last week.

"Really, it was silly. I am an atheist, member of the anti-God society at the university. But my mother had been ill, and I was poorly prepared for an English examination. So I prayed: 'O God, please help me in my examination.' Wasn't that silly?"

"Maybe not," I replied. "How did you do in examination?"

"Very well indeed," she answered. "My mind was clear, my memory worked well, and I received a good mark."

"Maybe the Lord helped you after all!"

"Sir," she retorted. "That is silly. I am an atheist and a member of the anti-God society, so, if there is a God, then surely he would know that I was his enemy. Why would he wish to help his enemy?"

"You live with your mother?"

She replied in the affirmative.

"You always do what your mother says?"

"No. I am an adult now. I make my own decisions."

"Sometimes you please your mother? Sometimes you grieve your mother?"

"That is true."

"But your mother still loves you? Why?"

"Well, she brought me into the world."

"God still loves you, even more."

She answered not a word, but I knew that the sword had gone home. I changed the subject. But, before we parted in the snow, she said to me:

"Where is this Evangelical Baptist Church? I would like to hear the choir sing sometime." That was as much as she dared say, for being reported as having betrayed an interest in religion could have cost her her job.

CHAPTER TWO

The Anatomy of Unbelief

In Kishinev, capital of the Republic of Moldavia, a Soviet junior official asked me, cordially:

"Have you learned any Russian, sir?"

"A little," I replied. "Twelve words."

"Twelve?" he asked, with a smile.

"Count them," said I. And I proceeded to say, in Russian, "Good morning," "Good evening," "Goodbye," "Tea with lemon," and "Thank you," adding the words "Slava Bogu."

"Slava Bogu," he echoed. "Where did you learn that?"

"Slava Bogu" is Russian for "Glory to God," an equivalent of "Praise the Lord." It is frequently used by believers.

"Is that not good Russian?" I asked.

"Very idiomatic," he assured me, "but old-fashioned."

"I learned that indirectly from Mr. Khrushchev."

"Mr. Khrushchev!"

"Yes, indeed. I have a friend who lived in Kansas City, in the middle of the United States. His mother had been born in Russia, but she was stone deaf. So my friend learned to lip-read Russian in order to help his mother.

"When Mr. Khrushchev visited United States," I went on, "my friend found that he could lip-read whatever he said in Russian on television. When Mr.

15

Khrushchev asked his interpreter, 'Who is that fat fool over there? Am I expected to shake hands with him?' he did not know that my friend was reading him clearly a thousand miles away.

"Someone in the crowd shouted in Russian, 'How is your health, Mr. Chairman?' Mr. Khrushchev looked for the owner of the Russian voice; then he beamed and said: 'Very good for a man of my years, praise the Lord!' using the Russian expression, 'Slava Bogu.'

"On another occasion," I continued, "someone shouted in Russian, 'What do you predict in Russian-American relations in the next ten years?' and Mr. Khrushchev replied: 'God only knows!'—using another pious Russian expression. My friend insisted that Mr. Khrushchev sounded very pious.

"In fact," I explained, "Mr. Khrushchev used such pious expressions that the Chinese Communists, who hated him, called him a Bible-quoting clown. Now, Mr. Khrushchev did not mind being called a clown, but he resented being called a Bible-quoting clown.

"So, I was told, he called together a conference of foreign newspaper men. 'Gentlemen of the press,' he announced, 'I wish to assure you that I am a convinced atheist.'

"An Englishman replied: 'You do talk a lot about the Almighty, sir, for an atheist.'

"Mr. Khrushchev frowned. He was unused to any hint of contradiction. Then he said, firmly:

" 'Must I tell you twice? I am chairman of the Council of Ministers of the Union of Soviet Socialist Republics, and I am an atheist.'

"A Frenchman asked, provocatively: 'How do we know that you are not a secret believer?'

"Mr. Khrushchev slammed the desk with his fist, and then he retorted:

" 'Will you listen to me? God knows I am an atheist.' "

Comrade Orgheyev smiled tolerantly.

"That was funny," he admitted, but he went on: "Very funny, but of course it did not mean anything. It was just conversation, just conversation."

"Granted, it was just conversation," I rejoined. "But it illustrates what I have discovered about atheists. Atheists are simply believers in reverse."

"Please?"

"Well, let me illustrate. I am Irish by birth, although I live in California. In Ireland, we have a certain minority, called Leprechauns . . ."

"Please?" he asked, more urgently.

"That's an Irish word, not English," I explained. "You cannot be expected to know it. Leprechauns are little fairy folk."

"Yes, yes," he agreed, eagerly. "We have that in Slavic folklore also— fairy people living in the forest."

"Well," said I. "I do not believe in Leprechauns. But I do not go around lecturing on 'Why I do not believe in the existence of Leprechauns.' Or, 'Leprechauns are not at all relevant to modern society.' Or, 'Leprechauns are dead.' I just leave Leprechauns alone. But atheists will not let God alone. They are obsessed with the idea of contradicting the idea of God. They spend their time justifying their unbelief. They are believers in reverse."

Unsubstantiated Atheism

My mind went back a quarter of a century or so, to D-Day on the Indonesian island of Morotai, where I was attached to the headquarters of the Thirteenth Air Force, advanced echelon. A pilot came to talk to me:

"Chaplain," he said. "I approve of the good work that you are doing, but I do not believe in it."

"Now what do you mean by that?" I asked.

"Some of these G.I.'s," he explained carefully, "get scared during an air raid, and they need a bit of religion to help them; but I'm an atheist, and I don't need any religion to help me at all!"

"Could I ask you a couple of questions?"

"Go ahead and shoot!" he agreed cheerfully.

"First," said I, "do you happen to know everything?"

"Of course not," he retorted. "Professor Albert Einstein said that scientists, as a whole, are on the fringe of knowledge. So I'll be quite modest and admit that I am on the fringe of the fringe!"

"Good," I commented. "The second question is this: Is it conceivable that God could exist outside all that you happen to know?"

He hesitated, so I asked facetiously:

"How much do you know?"

"How much what do I know?" he asked in reply.

"How much do you know, in relation to total knowledge? Ten percent?"

"Ten percent! Don't be ridiculous. Less than 1 percent! In fact, less than . . ."

"Well," I assured him, "let us just say 1 percent. Then is it possible that God could exist outside your 1 percent of knowledge?"

"Yes," he agreed. "Theoretically yes!"

"You're a most remarkable atheist then. Five minutes ago, you stated that there was no God, and now you say that it is possible there is one. Why don't you make up your mind?"

He returned a week later to explain.

"I have been thinking while I have been flying. No man really knows enough to be an atheist. To be an atheist you would really need to know everything, and if you knew everything, you could claim to be God yourself. The more I think about it, the more untenable philosophically it seems to be."

Five years later, I was researching at Oxford, where an Oxonian scholar, F. C. Copleston, arranged to debate the existence of God with Lord Bertrand Russell. The debate was broadcast by the BBC. At the outset, Lord Russell agreed quickly that the nonexistence of God cannot be proved, stating briefly, "My position is agnostic."[1] His convictions were atheistic—but he preferred to defend a less vulnerable position.

I have yet to hear any serious advocate attempt to prove a case for atheism. Instead, it is usual to listen to a suave attempt to discredit the scholastic arguments, as if the knowledge of God depended upon logic alone.

A returning tourist, asked to support his claim to citizenship, might produce only his driver's license. Rejection of his purported evidence would not constitute disproof of his citizenship, which might be established by other evidence in more convenient circumstances. Likewise, dismissal of the classic arguments for God as proof, while they still exhibit value as hypotheses derived from revelation, does not constitute a disproof of the existence of God.

Unsupported Skepticism

An atheist who denies the existence of God is forced to demonstrate that the revelation of God is incompatible with factual evidence and accepted truth. This he cannot do, so he must content himself with demolishing the medieval proofs of God's existence. A skeptic, on the other hand, who only doubts the possibility of the existence of God, is forced to show that the revelation of God is inferior in validity to substantiated alternatives. This he cannot do.

Irrelevant Agnosticism

Lieutenant Petersen, returning for another visit, had made it clear that he was no longer technically an atheist.

"I just used the wrong word," he said. "I'm not really an atheist. I'm an agnostic."

"Congratulations," I said.

"You like that?" said he.

"Yes, that's fine. Last week you said that you were an atheist—that God did not exist—but you could not prove this, so you were in a weak position. Now you say that you are an agnostic—you do not know if there is a God or not. You are in a stronger position, because you are telling the truth; you just don't know. The word *agnostic* comes from the Greek word *agnoo* and that means 'I do not know.' The word was used by Thomas Huxley to describe one who was not bold enough to deny the existence of God, but who found himself unconvinced by the arguments for God."[2]

Then I asked what kind of an agnostic he happened to be.

"Are there different kinds of agnostics?" he queried.

"Yes," I answered quickly, "there are two main kinds. Among Christians are Roman Catholics and Protestants. Among agnostics, there are two main denominations, the ordinary agnostics and the ornery ones."

"What do you mean by that?" he asked.

"The ordinary agnostic claims," I answered, " 'I do not know whether there is a God or not!' But the ornery one insists, 'I don't know, you don't know, nobody knows, and nobody ever will know!' I asked you what kind of an agnostic you may be because, if you say you know that I don't know, I'm going to ask you how you know that I don't know."

"Look here," said the pilot, "I quit right there. I'm a plain, ordinary agnostic. But what do you say about the arguments for ordinary agnosticism?"

"There aren't any!" I said, provocatively.

"What!" he retorted. "Professor Julian Huxley is a very brilliant scholar, and he's an agnostic."

"Granted," I agreed. "Professor Julian Huxley is one of the most brilliant experts in his field, in biology. But how could any man be brilliant in agnosticism, which means 'not-knowing-ness'? Long ago in Chicago, I took some hermeneutics courses. Do you know what hermeneutics is? No? Does Joe here know what hermeneutics is? No? Neither of you knows? Then which of the two is more brilliant in not knowing? You were good in physics, and Joe in mathematics, so which is more brilliant in not knowing hermeneutics?

"So what?" I went on. "Professor Julian Huxley is a brilliant man in biology, and says he is an agnostic, not knowing whether there is a God or not, so we consider that 'brilliant not-knowing'! Imagine one of your professors telling you after examinations: 'You're obviously clever in things you know least about, but you'll really brilliant in things you know nothing about!' When a

man says he does not know, he disqualifies himself."
Many will not accept the obvious disqualification.

Militant Agnosticism

The ornery or militant agnostic is much more difficult to debate. Only three years before that conversation, I had enrolled in a graduate course in historical
bibliography and criticism. The professor teaching that
class took ill and died, and the professor taking his
place called himself a secularist.

The professor was an agnostic, a militant one. Perhaps his belligerency was due to the fact that he had
been a reluctant candidate for the ministry, had taken a
bachelor of divinity degree, and had turned against religion entirely. He seemed to take a particular delight in
"picking on" believing Christians in his classes and
grilling them with red-hot questions.

When he found that he had an evangelist in his class,
he tried to have fun at my expense. He had given me a
paper to write on the topic, "The Influence of Geogra-
phy upon History," and I had said it was remarkable
that the world's three great revealed religions had
begun in the little land bridge between Europe, Asia,
and Africa, the middle of the land mass of the world.
This I thought a most significant fact in human history.
He objected.

"So, Orr," he commented. "You believe in God!" I
was quick to agree, but insisted that I had not intruded
that fact.

"Well, then, I want you to go to the blackboard. I
want you to diagram your beliefs. Put a dot on the

blackboard! And write your own initial O beside the dot."

As soon as I had obliged him, he asked me for a definition of science. I fumbled.

"Sir," I began, "science is—science is—we both know what science is!"

"Listen, Orr, I want to know what you think it is!"

I told him that I considered science to be the realm of proven fact or demonstrated knowledge. The professor accepted the word *knowledge*, and asked if there were limits to such knowledge. When this was agreed, he asked me to take chalk and draw a circle on the blackboard around the dot, theoretically enclosing all of Science, the realm of knowledge. I was then asked to give an example of a scientific fact. So I suggested that oxygen was 21 percent of the atmosphere. How did I know? I had demonstrated it in our physics laboratory.

"Agreed," said the professor. "Now, Orr, inside that circle is every known fact and item of knowledge. Is God inside that circle or outside?"

I suddenly realized that I was on the horns of a dilemma. If I claimed that God was within the circle of scientific knowledge, he would ask me to prove the existence of God the way one proves the existence of oxygen! That cannot be done. So I wrote the letter G outside the circle. The teacher was truly delighted. He repeated that God was outside the realm of knowledge —our accepted definition! He told me, with the heaviest of sarcasm, that almost anyone could think about God, could talk about God, could preach about God, could pray to God, but how could anyone really know God?

Not being much of a philosopher, I stood and stared

at the blackboard and the diagram forced upon me. While the class snickered, I began to reexamine the premises of the argument, and test the basic ideas. It suddenly struck me that I had been tricked into accepting wrong premises.

What right had he to make me put myself within the circle limited by science in the first place? I live in the middle of concentric circles of knowledge whose perimeters are drawn by the scientific method, the historical method, the legal method, and less exact systems of investigation and conclusion. The scientific method is invaluable for investigating matter, energy, and phenomena, but it possesses no competence in establishing events such as the murder of Julius Cæsar—there the historians are more competent. Scientists—experts in ballistics—may contribute details to the evidence of an armed robbery, but the legal method is much more competent in deciding the guilt of the accused. Scientists, lawyers, and historians defer to each other in their respective circles of competence, and most of them would concede that encompassing all of their overlapping circles are the perimeters of reality.

I am satisfied that I know God in my mind and heart by a historical revelation confirmed by personal experience. I took my chalk and extended the dot marked by my initial into an axis outside the circle of science, and linked it up with God by an arrow representing spiritual knowledge. In so doing, I had unwittingly diagrammed the statement of Christ that they who worship God must worship Him in spirit. Significantly, the Lord added "and in truth." What is truth? It may be more than scientific truth.

Uncertain Protheism

The agnostic has no case to prove. The skeptic, who only doubts the possibility of the existence of God, has an opposite number, the protheist, who admits the probability. The protheist has not carried his case far enough. Thus a sergeant whimsically commented:

"I believe there must be a God, but I don't think that the idea packs enough punch to motivate me. What does that make me? I am not an atheist, or an agnostic, or a skeptic."

"You have not taken the revelation of God seriously," I told him. "If you took it seriously enough, you would find it quite sufficient. You are a protheist. You concede the probability of the existence of God. That helps a little in the matter."

Inadequate Theism

The theist, whether he be Jew, Christian, or Muslim, affirms the existence of God. He needs only to show that the revelation is compatible with the evidence. The most vocal atheist of my acquaintance, a well-trained debater, stated simply: "The doctrine of theism, the belief in the existence of God, offers us what is at first sight the most plausible account of some of the most pervasive, exciting, and extraordinary aspects of our existence and our environment." His second sight involved the most complicated sophistry. Our knowledge of God comes to us by divine revelation; but it is congenial to reason, and it is a very persuasive hypothesis. No atheist has shown it to be at all incompatible with the evidence, no skeptic that it is inferior in validity to its alternatives; the agnostic is not qualified to pronounce judgment; the revelation is not only superior in validity, as a protheist would admit, but it is compatible with the evidence, as a theist may confidently contend.

But it is not enough to be a theist. Many a theist has had no personal experience of God. To him, God is only a proposition, a hypothesis. The truth in Christ Jesus must reveal Him as a loving Father.

A Christian Case

In the earliest part of the century, before the days of he Republic, an Irishman was taking a shortcut across he estate of an English Duke, when whom should he ncounter but the Duke himself.

"My good man," said the Duke, "you are tres-assing."

"Am I that, now?" retorted Murphy.

"This is my property," said the Duke.

"And where did you get it?" asked Murphy.

"From my father," answered the Duke.

"And where did he get it?"

"From my grandfather," replied the Duke.

"And where did he get it?" asked the conversation-list.

"From my ancestors, you impertinent bounder."

"And where did they get it?" asked Murphy.

"They fought for it," replied the Duke, proudly.

Whereupon Murphy raised his fists, remarking:

"I'll fight ye for it."

Others have fought for their rights and won, but some have fought for their rights and lost, Magyars and Czechs in turn capitulating to superior force in recent years. The rights of all men, not only Americans, to life and liberty and the pursuit of happiness were attributed by Thomas Jefferson in 1776 to God, their Creator, and this was called "a self-evident truth."

27

General Awareness

What is a self-evident truth? It is a truth that appeal to common sense, a truth that need not be proved to the ordinary man, though sophistic philosophers migh quibble over it.[1] What is an example of a self-eviden truth? The axiom of self-existence—"I believe I exist you believe you exist; they believe they exist—is there anyone not sure?" Indeed, I have met with some who doubted such an axiom but all were philosophers who had once believed it.

There was once a Chinese philosopher who dreamed that he was a butterfly, and, when he awakened, the dream was so vivid that he did not know whether he was a man dreaming that he was a butterfly, or a butter-fly dreaming that he was a man. Some oriental sages have taught that life is an illusion, and it is certainly true that human beings are the prisoners of their five senses.

One of our planes crashed at Morotai, and I went to pray with the dying and to bury the dead. One poor fellow was wrapped in bandages to the tip of his nose; I did not know whether he was Jewish, Roman Catholic or Protestant, but I wished to offer him some comfort so I asked: "May I read to you the Twenty-third Psalm?" He did not answer, so I began to read. In the course of my reading, he called out:

"Hey, Doc! Open the window, Doc. It's awful stuffy.'

The poor lad was out in the open air; he had lost his sight; he had lost his hearing; presumably, he had lost his sense of taste and sense of smell; he was losing his sense of touch, being under heavy sedation. He soon lapsed into a coma from which he never recovered What could life mean to him? Life could be a dream but we assume it to be true—a self-evident truth that we do not attempt to prove.

The acceptance of the self-evident truth of God seems to be a general human intuition. When the first Europeans arrived on the North American continent, they found a noble savage, reverencing the sun, the moon and stars, the wind and weather—but he had a word for God, the Great Spirit. In New Guinea, I went on patrol in the densest jungle with primitive Papuans, and found that they had an intuition of a Supreme Being, for animists worldwide possess a distinct awareness of a Great Creator and Sustainer along with an abject appeasement of malign demonic forces.[2]

The early Vedic writings indicate a Hindu intuition of the Supreme Being, corrupted later into pantheism and a pantheon of lesser gods reflecting human passion and frailty, as in the legends of the Greeks and Germans. Buddhists usually are technical agnostics but practical theists—as anyone visiting the shrine of the goddess of mercy in Tokyo must realize. And in the modern communistic states, the natural theistic tendencies of the people are suppressed only by the most sustained of all persecutions, backed by a systematic anti-religious indoctrination that tolerates no hearing of the alternatives. Under fire, my atheistic comrades swore or prayed negative or positive invocations of Almighty God.

Divine Revelation

I was speaking at an international student banquet when a Japanese girl raised her hand and said,

"Sir, isn't one man's idea of God just as good as another man's idea of God?"

"I'll have to answer you by asking a question," I replied. "I was married in Africa thirty years ago. What do you think my wife looks like?"

"I don't know," she said.

"Well, have a guess. I won't grade you on your answer."

"Is she brunette?" she asked.

"What else?"

"Dark eyes?"

"What else?"

"Short?"

"Why short?"

"Why, shorter than you are."

"Are you sure of all this?" I asked.

"I'm guessing, sir. You told me to guess."

Then I turned to another person and said,

"What do you think my wife looks like?"

"Well," he replied, "just to be different, I'll say that she's blonde, blue-eyed, and the same size as you."

I asked another person's opinion and got a different answer. So I said:

"Can we get together on this? Do we all agree that her ideas are no better than his ideas, that what he says is no better than what the third person says?"

We all agreed. So I turned to the Japanese girl and asked her briskly:

"Would you like to know what my wife looks like?"

"You've made me curious," she replied.

"Her parents were Norwegian," I explained, "She's a natural blonde. Her eyes are grey-blue. She spent eighteen years in the African sun, so she has freckles. She weighs a hundred and thirty-five pounds; she's five feet five inches."

"Would you say that my idea is no better than your

idea and what I said is no better than what he said?" I
asked.

"That's not fair, sir," she replied, "that's not fair.
You told us to guess."

"Well, what about me? Am I not guessing?"

"No," she answered, "you're informing us."

"But," I asked, "why do you take my word for it?"

"I have every reason to believe it," she assured me.

"Now, listen," I explained. "The prophets of old did
not declare, 'There must be somebody upstairs that
likes me.' Moses said, 'God spoke these words' and he
gave us the Ten Commandments, which are the basis of
our civilization. David said, 'The Lord is my shepherd,
I shall not want.' Ezekiel said, 'The word of the Lord
came unto me the second time.' But Jesus Christ gave
us the unsurpassed revelation of God when He said,
'He that hath seen me hath seen the Father.'[3]

"It's your privilege to reject these things, but be hon-
est. They were not speculating; they claimed to know.
It was a divine revelation, which you are free to reject.
That is your privilege."

"How do you know all this?" asked the Japanese
girl.

"You read it in a little book called the New Testament."

"My folks are Buddhist, and in Buddhism we have
certain legends. How do I know that the New Testament is not just legend?"

"You must not have read it," I replied. "In the third
chapter of the Gospel of Luke, it says, 'In the fifteenth
year of Tiberius Cæsar, when Pontius Pilate was governor of Judea and Herod prince of Galilee . . .
Caiaphas and Annas being the high priests . . .' Histori-
cally, there are seven checkpoints for the scholars.[4]

"If a hundred years from now somebody wrote, 'In the second term of Franklin Roosevelt as president of the United States, while Ronald Reagan was governor of California, and John Lindsay mayor of New York City,' any historian could easily tear that statement apart, for when Franklin Roosevelt was president, Ronald Reagan was not governor of California, nor John Lindsay mayor of New York City.

"The New Testament is one of the best attested ancient documents of all time. When I was in college thirty or forty years ago, it was taught that the Gospel of John was written in the late second century: that was the consensus of scholars. William Albright of Johns Hopkins University, a leading archaeologist until his death, said recently that he was satisfied that the Gospels were completed before 85 A.D.[5] The Apostle Paul wrote to the Corinthians about 55 A.D., 'There are still more than four hundred people alive who actually saw Christ after His resurrection.' "[6]

Our knowledge of God comes to us by divine revelation. It is not a philosophical speculation.

Human Reason

My son, David, before he trained as a jet pilot, worked his way through his university courses in political science by operating computers in a data-processing organization. This made me curious about computers, which the layman holds in awe. Believe it or not, I persuaded a professor to let me enroll in an advanced course for teachers, listed as Curriculum for Computers, without the prerequisites of undergraduate and graduate classes in the subject. I never enjoyed a course more.

In the last class, after examinations, I asked:

"Professor, would you agree that a seventeen-year-old girl could be taught to program a computer?"

"Oh, yes," he replied, "if she can punch cards, she can program a computer."

"But," said I, "that does not mean that she can write the program."

"No," he agreed, "but she could transcribe it into the computer."

"If the machine broke down, she could not repair it?"

"No. A technician would be needed to do that."

"And she could not build another computer?"

"No," he agreed, "an engineer would have to do that."

"Wouldn't you agree then that human conception is a kind of program? A young couple get married, decide to have a baby. Each contributes twenty-three chromosomes, which carry the genes which decide whether the baby will have long fingernails or blue eyes and so forth. This takes about two hundred and eighty days. Where does the program come from?"

"Not from the young couple," he answered mischievously. "They just punch the cards!"

"Then, where does it come from?"

"Get away with you, Orr," he replied. "That's theology."

I have a friend in Los Altos who has an IQ of 208. (Albert Einstein's IQ was 209). Dr. Gerhard Dirks, consultant in computers, told me that it was possible to build a computer that could play chess. But it is not an economical proposition, for a teenager can play chess less expensively. Dirks tried to work out the number of bits of information to account for the human brain. It was so fantastic that he was forced to choose between chance and Providence to explain it. Once he was willing to give Providence some consideration, it was not long before he found God in Christ.

Cybernetics, computer science, is one of the youngest scientific disciplines, and many of my friends in computer work have found their Christian faith confirmed thereby—not the only scientists to agree. A brilliant professor of mathematics at a leading university told me:

"Whoever or whatever is responsible for mathematical order in the universe is one unique genius in mathematics."

The hypothesis of a Designer of the universe is stronger than ever in these days of expansion of scientific knowledge. And what can be said of the teleological hypothesis—the argument from design—can be said of the cosmological hypothesis—the argument from beginnings—and of the anthropological hypothesis—the argument from morality.

It is fashionable to disregard the classical arguments for Christianity. Aquinas's arguments, after making a case for the prime mover and a case for the first cause, jump a gap by saying of the conclusion: "And we agree that this is God," a step of faith, not a conclusive argument. But in the hurry to abandon the arguments, some forget that they are still good as hypotheses, though not as proofs. It is quite possible on a blackboard to demonstrate that the square of the hypotenuse of a right-angle triangle is equal to the sum of the squares on the other two sides. But no one can ever demonstrate God by such logical entailment. Neither can anyone demonstrate self-existence thereby.

The hypothesis of God still provides the most satisfactory answer to the problem of cosmology, of teleology, and of anthropology. Our knowledge of God is congenial to reason, on every count.

Personal Experience

An awareness of God comes to us through a general human intuition. But knowledge of God comes to us through divine revelation; it is congenial to reason; and it may be verified through personal experience.

Some personal experience is common to the human race. Some is the experience of minorities. I met a fellow who was addicted to hard drugs, and he told me:

"LSD makes red a bright scarlet; it makes blue a deep, deep blue. Sometimes you feel as if you're soaring away up in the sky; other times you feel as if you're coming down a roller coaster. It sharpens all your perceptions; you're out of this world."

"You mean that you're out of your mind?" I asked.

"It could be dangerous," he admitted.

"Dangerous," I echoed. "It has caused murder and rape and assault and suicide and robbery and all sorts of bizarre conduct. A fellow on drugs at UCLA decided he was a bird and jumped out of a fifth-story window in the dormitory. Instead of going up like a bird, he came down like a rock! He landed on a thorn bush, which sharpened all his perceptions, of course."

The experiences of drug addicts are not held in question. I have never taken LSD in my life, but I believe that it causes hallucinations. If that is true, then, who can really disregard Christian experience, supported by the testimony of some of the world's most trustworthy characters.

An opponent in debate told me:

"I do not disregard Christian experience. Some fellow whom everyone knows is all mixed up goes to hear Billy Graham and gets straightened out. I approve of that, but I can explain it psychologically."

Sirhan Sirhan was charged with the murder of Robert Kennedy. A psychiatrist defending him declared that the reason why he murdered Robert Kennedy was that he loved his own mother, but hated his father, and transferred the hatred of his father to Robert Kennedy, hence he murdered Robert Kennedy. Therefore, he was not to blame.

A psychiatrist for the prosecution contradicted every word he said. What could a jury do? They convicted Sirhan on the evidence of his diary.

Some people think they can explain Christian experience. Why not go to the people who experienced it! They explain it by the same divine revelation that told them about God, told them that they are sinners, that they needed to repent and turn to God and be converted.

There is a knowledge that defies a glib explanation. It is, of course, difficult to illustrate such a personal awareness. I know that my wife loves me but I do not think that I could prove it to everyone who challenged me. But I do not need to prove it thus in order to enjoy the relationship. It would be nice to think that all and sundry fully agreed that the Orrs were a happily married couple, but such a foolproof demonstration is superfluous. I can recommend the relationship to others, provided they accept the rules involved in happy matrimony. Neither I nor my friends who follow suit need to prove it to those who deny it; their agreement may be desirable, but it is not necessary for the already convinced.

And that is the wonder of personal faith in God. Any believer can know without being able to persuade someone who does not want to know, and that is the crux of the matter—the questioner must become a seeker before becoming a finder. Seek, and the promise guarantees finding.

But the finder is always anxious to share his knowledge. It is not like membership in an exclusive club. Furthermore, there is an obligation to answer honest questions. It has the force of a commandment.

"Always be ready to give a logical reply to the one who asks you for a reason of the hope that is within you," said the Apostle Peter.[7] That gives a warrant for apologetics; and it is declared in the Letter to the Hebrews:

"Without faith, it is impossible to please God. He who comes to God must first believe that He exists and that He rewards those who diligently seek Him." That gives the invitation to faith.

CHAPTER FOUR

The Cosmological Argument

A friend of mine, who did not care much for the drinking crowd in the officers' club, spent a lot of his time trying to improve his skill at the game of pool. Even when he could find no competitor, he endlessly practiced caroming one ball off another. Dropping into the pocket was a red ball, which had been struck by a green ball, hit by a blue ball, bumped by a yellow ball, slammed by a purple ball, smacked by an orange ball, knocked by a black ball, banged by a white ball—each traced back to the cue in the hand of the player, moved by the muscles, motivated by the mind of the ardent lieutenant, that mind being the prime mover or first cause.

Thinking men, since twenty centuries or more ago, have often pondered the continuous motion in this world, one thing causing another. The idea of an infinite regress—one thing being caused by another endlessly—staggered their minds.

Summarizing, the Greek philosopher Plato taught that the power to produce motion logically precedes the power to receive such motion and to pass it on; that, in transmitting change, there must first be an uncaused cause to originate the motion. "How can a thing which is moved by another ever be the beginning of change?" he asked.[1] In Plato's view, the ultimate cause of all movement in the universe must be a living soul of a higher order than a human soul. And he then defined *soul* as the motion which can move itself. *Force* would be a more acceptable word to use today, for *soul* is suggestive of something more than motion and cause.

Aristotle, the pupil of Plato, argued that change itself suggested an ultimate unchanging source of movement, for as each thing moved is moved by another mover, the very last member of this series must of necessity be ungenerated, seeing that something cannot come from nothing.[2] Aristotle's philosophy was rediscovered in the thirteenth century, and greatly influenced the thinking of medieval scholars.

The Thomistic Assumption

The greatest of the medieval Roman Catholic thinkers—St. Thomas Aquinas—presented the cosmological argument under three headings in his five proofs of the existence of God. They may be simply stated.[3]

First, he argued that everything which is moved must be moved by another, and that, to avoid an infinite regress in this chain of movers, the existence of a first unmoved mover must be conceded. Second, he argued that everything which is caused must be caused by something else, and that in this hierarchy of efficient causes, again rejecting an infinite regress of causes, there must be a first efficient cause. And, in the third instance, he argued that, as some things come into the world and then cease to be, it is possible for such things either to exist or not to exist—their own existence is not a necessity. Aquinas argued further that it is impossible for things of this sort to exist forever, seeing that whatever is capable of not existing actually does not exist at some time or other. Therefore, if all things were of this transient sort, allowing the hypothesis of limitless time, at some time there would be nothing; and thus if ever there were nothing in existence, nothing would now exist, for no thing is capable of bringing itself into existence. Hence, there must be something that is always existing. In all three instances, Aquinas jumped from his conclusion—of a prime mover, a first cause, or a necessary being—to God, assuming general agreement.[4]

In succeeding centuries, there were scholars who fancied the Thomist arguments as invincible. The rationalist, David Hume, a friend of the French revolutionists, assaulted these accepted proofs with severity. The cosmological argument he dismissed as an absurdity pretending to demonstrate a matter of fact. The term *necessary existence* in his view had no meaning, and in any case, why should not the material universe itself be the necessarily existent being?[5] As this objection has been maintained by skeptics ever since, it is deserving of close consideration.

Laymen today also find the idea of an infinite regress of movers or causes repugnant to their common sense, but not so some modern philosophers, whose minds seem to be capable of feats of acrobatics which laymen find hard to follow. Their sophistry must be considered.

Avoiding a Proper Question

The gist of the objections raised in most debates is this: The skeptic asks: "Where did the universe come from?" The Christian replies: "From God." The skeptic inquires: "And where does God come from?"[6] And the Christian answers: "That is not a proper question, because God by definition is eternal." However, if the Christian may reject the question: "Where did God come from?" as not a proper question, why cannot a skeptic reject the question: "Where did the universe come from?" as not a proper question?

This is the line taken by Bertrand Russell in his debate with F. C. Copleston. It is proper, thought Russell, to ask the question of the cause of the existence of all particular objects, but improper to ask the question of the cause of the existence of the total of all of them. Said he:

"I should say that the universe is just there and that's all."[7] And he affirmed that it was illegitimate to ask the question of the cause of the world, whereupon his opponent declared: "If one refuses even to sit down at the chessboard and make a move, one cannot of course be checkmated."

"Have you stopped beating your wife?"—not a proper question—can be restated in court as "Have you ever or do you now beat your wife?" Let us restate the question.

The question: "Where did the universe as human beings observe it today come from?" has been answered by the astronomers. The consensus of astronomers accepts the idea of an expanding universe which began with "a big bang" so many thousands of million years ago. And the idea of an infinite regress of movers and causes is implicit in the notion that the universe "has always been there"—which offers no hint of an explanation for the principle of entropy, as seen in the second law of thermodynamics.[8]

Richard Feynman, professor of physics at California Institute of Technology, a Nobel Prize winner in his field, asked if the laws of physics are reversible and answered his own question: "Evidently not. Just try to unscramble an egg! . . . The most natural characteristic

of all phenomena is their obvious irreversibility."[9] So
says revelation also.

Lay people find the laws of thermodynamics difficult
to comprehend. I heard a soldier illustrate from gambling:

"You never get something for nothing—that's the
first law; you don't even break even—that's the second
law."

The second law is "time's arrow" for the reactions
that take place in nature.[10] We have every reason to
believe that our universe is a closed system, and no
evidence apparent that it is not—for neither steady-
state cosmology nor the theory of a fluctuating universe
has produced any evidence—which all suggests that the
universe is not a continuous machine; there must have
been a point at which it began to decline.[11] Must not a
superior power have organized it?

The objector raises another point: the universe must
include everything that ever was and is, therefore must
also include God. Again a stalemate is reached, for the
theist objects that of course God did not create Himself
thus.

Refuters, from David Hume and his disciples to Bertrand Russell and his followers, nowhere attempted to
disprove at all the existence of God,[12] only to disqualify the arguments. Russell dismissed the cosmological
argument by insisting that the universe is the only abid-
ing reality; whereas "What we call the world is intrinsi-
cally unintelligible, apart from the existence of God,"
was Copleston's rejoinder to this idea. The cosmological argument has required a premise that is refused by
the very people to whom it is directed, who deny the
reality of the problem, affirm that things that exist simply exist and that their origin is a pseudoquestion.

Presenting a Proper Hypothesis

The only alternative, therefore, to offering the argument of cosmology as a proof or demonstration is to present it as a persuasive hypothesis, not a logical certainty. Contrasted with the explanations of the origin of the universe presented by its opponents, it demonstrates a superior kind of reasonableness. Opponents state that it is equally likely that the universe is itself eternal. The consensus of opinion among modern scientists is that the observable universe came into existence several billion years ago, and the second law of thermodynamics postulates that the universe, since its beginning, has been running down, that this law of entropy is something that nature cannot reverse. The argument of a prime mover, a first cause, a necessary being, is far more harmonious with scientific conclusions than its alternatives.

The cosmological argument thus does not disprove that the universe is eternal, but affirms that the revelation of God as Creator provides a hypothesis which is compatible with all the evidence offered by sense and science.[13]

CHAPTER FIVE

The Teleological Argument

In the 1930s, I was traveling around the British Isles on a bicycle, and had occasion to send a telegram to my mother at home in Ireland. So I approached the counter in a telegraph office, asked for a telegram form, wrote out my message and handed it to the attendant, who then counted the number of words, calculated the charges, accepted my payment, and dispatched the telegram. The telegram was given to a telegraphist who, using a series of binary electrical impulses to convey the letters of the words of the message in Morse code, transferred the telegram to a central office from which it was dispatched to the place addressed. There another telegraphist converted the sounds made by these electrical impulses into letters and words, composed the message and its address, wrote it on a form and dispatched a messenger boy with the telegram to my boyhood home.

It seemed obvious to me, even in those days, that to operate a telegraph system, a certain amount of planning and organization was necessary. Someone had to print the telegram forms, and someone had to place them on the rack. Someone had to build the telegraph office, and someone had to train the telegraphists to use the Morse code that someone had to invent. Someone had to erect telegraph poles and someone had to string the telegraph wires. Someone had to design the receiving sets as well as the transmitters. And someone had to hire the telegram delivery boys, as well as provide them with bicycles. It seemed inconceivable that a telegraph system had just occurred without intelligent plan.

The human nervous system resembles a telegraph system. If someone sticks a pin into your leg, a chain of nerve cells conveys a message to your brain, saying "Murphy, you have been stabbed!" Another message is sent to the vocal cords, directing them to say: "Ah!" It is very difficult for any ordinary human being to believe that nerve cells, following only a law of nature, should link themselves into chains of great length to receive and pass on such messages to the brain. What would make them do so?

Apparently, this is regarded as a proper question by the sophisticated skeptics. The order in nature cannot be denied but design can be disputed.

There are those who attribute the phenomena of life to chance. I have heard it said, but have not comprehended the logic, that "the very fact that I am here is proof that chance produced me." This is no more proof that chance produced this specious speculator than that such a person was evolved by the music of the Greek god, Pan.[1]

Random Chance?

Everything began by chance? But few realize the odds. When dice are tossed, the chance of getting a six is one out of six; twice running—one out of 36; three times running—one out of 216; four times running—one out of 1,296; twelve times running—one out of 2,176,782,336. What would be the chance to get dice to roll the same way all the time? It is fantastic.

The story is told of an Oxford professor who believed that a team of monkeys typing on a set of type-writers sooner or later would strike off all the great classics of literature, including Shakespeare.[2]

No scholar so brilliant would waste his time supervising so tedious an experiment, so the professor arranged for members of his philosophy class to make the necessary arrangements for a dozen monkeys to spend eight hours a day typing on a dozen typewriters.

In the seventeenth year of the project, a Merton College man called the professor to make his daily report. A monkey was dead, another ill, one was antisocial, the others typing. "No, sir," he explained. "They do not type individual words, let alone sentences. And one monkey goes around tearing up what the others type. But, this morning at 8:16, there was something exceptional. One monkey typed the following sentence: 'To be, or not to be, that is the unzin-quatch.' "

The extreme unlikelihood of any such achievement may be facetiously demonstrated. Any typist could manage with thirty keys on the keyboard.[3] The chance of getting the first letter right is 1 in 30; the second, 1 in 900; of getting two words of ten letters in all, 1 in 30 to the tenth power, or 1,771,470,000,000,000. If all the monkeys on earth were employed as typists since the world began, there would be little probability of accidentally composing Hamlet.

At the University of Washington, I gave an illustration of chance in the rolling of dice. A scientist approached me afterwards and commented:

"Orr, your illustration about the dice is interesting but quite unnecessary. In physics, statistically speaking, there is no such thing as chance."

And that is so. Hydrogen burned with oxygen produces water. Combined a hundred times, it produces water one hundred times. Combined a million times, it produces water a million times. It is true that physicists cannot tell which atoms of uranium will deteriorate by radioactivity into lead, but statistically they can predict how many will do so, and how long it will take. The hydrogen bomb is a result of random collisions of nuclear particles involving "chance" results, yet the reliability of the process is seen in the amount of energy released by the sun every second in known time, so that tiny variations are predicted in spite of the enormous number of nuclear collisions occurring. Sunburn is considered constant in history.

It is interesting that the language employed by scientists working in the laboratory often differs from that used when reference is made to historical events. Thus, a geneticist describing current experiments will speak of fixed mutation rates, whereas in speculating about these factors in past evolution, he refers to chance mutations. Why are present and demonstrable mutations described in terms of law, and those past considered accidents? Surely the answer lies in the philosophy in which the scientist is indoctrinated? His philosophy interprets the past, not the present.

Pierre Lecomte du Noüy set forth an argument purporting to show that chance could not account for development of life on earth.[4] But, as the director of Oak Ridge Nuclear Institute, W. G. Pollard, pointed out, his arguments make an improper use of scientific results in their treatment of probability.[5] It is equally fallacious to suggest that the process of life is the result of chance, for chance in itself cannot be a causative agent. Yet sciolists have pontificated that "man is the result of a purposeless and materialistic process that did not have him in mind. He was not planned," which is something that such a cocksure writer could not know.

Chance is suggested to explain order while denying design; but the laws of nature are cited to explain utility in nature while denying purpose. Purpose is not so easily dismissed.

Utility and Purpose

When I visited India, Sir Julian Huxley lectured there and declared: "Out of a purposeless universe has come man with purpose." This is something that neither Sir Julian nor anyone else could speak of with assurance. It is pure speculation, and it does not make sense.

In my youth, I played soccer. Well I knew that chance events would bring the ball some time to my feet, but it was not chance that enabled me to score a goal—it was purpose. The trajectory of the ball, of course, followed the laws of nature.

The laws of nature, of course, are cited when convenient by unbelievers, but none attempts to suggest an answer to the question of the origin of these laws. They are as old as the universe, and the question of their establishment is as interesting as that of the origin of the material universe. For some, it is highly convenient to dismiss the question.

Of course, philosophers are found who relentlessly rebut the notion of purpose in nature. That is just the way the laws of nature operate, they say: it is not a matter of simple chance, and certainly not an evidence of providence.

Thus a brilliant atheist of my acquaintance illustrated purposelessness in natural law by pointing out that in many limestone caverns iciclelike objects project from the roof and build up again from the floor. That stalagmites are always found directly under stalactites, he asserted, should never be attributed to either chance or plan.[6] The illustration was singularly inept, for what theist postulates a plan?

Of course, there seem to be designs in nature which do not appear to be purposeful. A compound of hydrogen and oxygen dropping from a cloud in freezing air invariably forms snowflakes in the most exquisite patterns, exciting the envy of artists and the wonder of mathematicians, the former affirming that only artistic genius could duplicate the variety of design, the latter insisting that mathematical genius alone could devise such formulæ in mathematical terms. Why such laws of nature should exceed the genius of man is utterly astounding. Hence artists and mathematicians known to me attribute such a marvel to Intelligence that far exceeds the ingenuity of any man or indeed of all men put together; but never once do any of them hint at any kind of usefulness in the beauty of a snowflake.

Man sometimes has found a usefulness for properties of things, as (for example) in the diamond which is so hard that it is used to cut glass and to drill much harder things. But no one suggests that diamonds were so designed to help friendly glaziers in cutting window panes.

Purposeful Complexity

But all simplistic explanations seem so unsatisfactory when it comes to the complexities of the human body.[7] Take, for example, the human eye. The eyeball in diameter is about an inch, but its light-sensitive layer or retina is less than a millimeter thick. Yet the retina contains a hundred million elements sensitive to light, whose bits of information are fed through a complex computer within the retina itself and integrated into messages of hue, tone, tint, shade, shape, and texture which are relayed by a million fibered nerves to the brain for further assessment. It is obvious that the eye could not have been something that some apt ancestor of an ape discovered useful. For natural selection, the eye must have been efficient at the outset, or it would never have been selected in the first place.

A tape cassette with too much background noise can cause despair to the keenest listener. The human ear has such a sensitivity that it is able to detect a sound so faint that the eardrum vibrates a fraction of the width of a single molecule of hydrogen. If it were more sensitive, a constant background noise would drive us to distraction.

Take digestion. To utilize the simplest food substance, sugar, the stomach passes it through a series of dozens of chemical transformations, each of which is achieved by use of highly complex enzymes, the lack of one of which can bring the chain of reactions to a standstill. Carbon, as an element, possesses such unique properties suited to the structure and function of living organisms that it is very difficult not to postulate purpose to explain utility.

The Argument from Design

But long before the scientists discovered such surprises, design in nature caught the notice of philosophers. The classic illustration of the argument for God was given by William Paley, the apologist.[8] In simple words, a stroller may strike his foot against a stone upon a heath, and is unlikely to be perplexed to explain the finding of anything so lacking in complexity. But, if he were to discover a watch, he would not be easily satisfied to conclude that the watch also developed by fortuitous circumstance. The mechanism of the watch is clearly seen to demonstrate a purpose; in fact, the individual parts themselves so demonstrate such purpose that one must conclude that the watch possessed a maker. The observer might never have seen a watch made, might discover that the watch was keeping time erratically, and might also be unable to explain the purpose of several of its parts; yet he would find it hard to believe that the assembling of the watch was just a possible combination of sundry parts, that it followed a principle of order, and that it was due to the laws of nature, therefore he should accept it as a fact and not jump to conclusions. So said Paley who claimed that only God could be designer of wonders found in nature —a conclusion that did not necessarily follow.

The argument of design, even before Paley published his version of it, received severest criticism from David Hume and has continued to receive rebuttal until present times. "Were this world ever so perfect a production," said Hume, "it must still remain uncertain whether all the excellences of the work can justly be ascribed to the workman."[9]

What an exalted idea one must form of the ingenuity of the carpenter who framed so complicated, so useful and so beautiful a vessel as a sailing ship. Then one of surprise to find him a stupid navvy who imitated others and copied a blueprint slowly improved after many trials, mistakes and corrections, deliberations, and controversies—thus Hume!

So it is obvious that Hume's ship, like Paley's watch, is produced by a collection of intelligent makers. The argument from design does not prove the existence of an infinite God, but admits the possibility of either a less-than-infinite being or a collection of Gods. Hence, the teleological argument must call on other sources of knowledge to rebut the idea of a lesser creator or demiurge or of a whole company of gods on Mount Olympus. It simply postulates Intelligence of a supernatural order to account for design.[10]

The Scottish skeptic did not disprove superior Intellect. Hume agreed that an intelligent being of such vast power and capacity needed to produce the universe would exceed all analogy and even comprehension; this a Christian would readily accept, for he derives his limited ideas of God from divine self-revelation, not from speculation or analogy.

Recently, an able debater presented me with a more up-to-date rebuttal of the validity of the watch and watchmaker argument, using similar terms. A Swiss scientist, hearing the watch illustration, volunteers: "I'll show you how watches are made today." And he takes his friend to a completely automated Swiss watch factory, where machines without any human direction are mechanically producing parts and fitting them together, unprocessed materials entering the factory on a belt and finished articles coming off the production line. That certainly seemed to be a fair analogy of the scientific view of the operations of our automated world of nature.

But the analogy has its weaknesses. It does not pretend to explain where the original materials came from, where the project was planned, or what sustained the operation. If the automated workings were projected and controlled by a sophisticated computer, the necessity of accounting for an even more wonderful mechanical marvel is raised, the mind that planned the computer being more highly rated than the mind of a watchmaker. It certainly does not discredit the argument for some kind of designer. The hypothesis of a designer remains effective and useful.

A Better Explanation?

Some find the argument fallacious because they offer "a better explanation of order," namely the operation of evolution easily supported by evidence[11]—"we can even demonstrate the evolutionary process in a laboratory," a staggering claim. Of course, some steps in development can be demonstrated; the most significant cannot; and no one explains the why!

Few informed students do not accept the conclusions of qualified scientists regarding the sequential appearance of life on this planet. There was a time when primitive life left no traces in the rocks, followed by a time when only the shells of trilobites and the like were deposited; then vertebrate fish contributed skeletons; then amphibians and reptiles, birds, mammals, and man. It is quite another thing to say that any scientist proves that this was accomplished by random chance, for even those who so affirm certainly cannot prove by any scientific method that this was so.

It has also been claimed that the steps in the evolution of inorganic chemicals into organisms can be demonstrated as products of random chance in the interplay of properties of matter. This is far from the case.

Steps can be demonstrated, not chance. Miller and Urey passed a charge of electricity, simulating light-

ning, through a cloud of methane and ammonia—
representing the earth's earliest atmosphere[12]—and
found amino acids in the residue; amino acids are the
building blocks of proteins and proteins the building
blocks of life; therefore could life have begun by
chance? But this is no more an argument for atheistic
spontaneous evolution than for deistic or theistic mediate evolution. And the production of amino acids by
lightning ages ago is no more an argument against God
than is the production of nitrogen compounds, ferti-
lizers in the fields, by lightning in today's atmosphere of
nitrogen and oxygen. A theistic explanation can be
given such demonstrated steps, as Professor Urey readily conceded in this case.

Again, it should be noted that refuters of the teleological argument, from David Hume and his disciples to
Bertrand Russell and his contemporaries, nowhere attempted to disprove the existence of God, only to disqualify the arguments. "Could there have been a Designer?" asked Michael Scriven. "Indeed there could, if
by this we mean a Being which gave form to all the
Universe and which derived its own form from nothing
outside itself."[13] "Belief in the existence of God offers
us what at first sight is the most plausible account of
some of the most pervasive, exciting, and extraordinary
aspects of our existence."[14] Then he rejects the idea on
the ground that it does not answer the question of the
origin of the Designer. But the Christian has the answer
to that very question. Divine revelation has conveyed
the truth that the Designer (and Creator) of the universe is eternal, as His name in French affirms, and this
revelation treated as a proper hypothesis has never
been invalidated.

Presenting a Proper Hypothesis

The teleological argument also has required a premise that is refused by the people to whom it is offered. Hence, instead of presenting it as a proof or demonstration, it should be advanced as a persuasive hypothesis.

CHAPTER SIX

The Anthropological Argument

"To me," said the fellow from Adelaide, "man is nothing more than matter in a highly organized form."

He threw another stick in the fire, and the pungent smell of burning eucalyptus wood invaded our nostrils. We were sitting by a campfire in Arnhem Land, Northern Australia, all of us from New South Wales except an aborigine tracker, the university student from South Australia, and me.[1]

"I suppose," said I, "that you would call yourself, if not a Marxist, a scientific humanist."

Kevin agreed, insisting that man was nothing more than an accidental by-product of physical and chemical forces, lacking any purpose for his own existence or any future at all beyond the grave.

One of the missionaries from Sydney spoke his piece, saying that, on the contrary, he believed that man is rather a spirit, living for a time in a material body, the present life a training ground for an eternal destiny.

"I know you do, padre," said Kevin. "But I do not, and you'll have a hard time convincing me. But this I'll say, you and I have a lot in common. You are up here to help the *abos*, and so am I. I want to do all I can to promote their health and happiness, and to push their economic and cultural development without upsetting their ways too much."

"Kevin," said I, "all of us are appreciative of the work that you are doing. You're a sort of one-man Peace Corps. But you make me curious. Why should you work for the good of mankind?"

"Why not?" he retorted. "I've got to show the wowsers back in Adelaide that you don't need to be a Bible-thumper to do good!"

"You misunderstand me," I replied. "I don't mean why you, in particular, but why you or anybody? If man is only the accidental by-product of physical and chemical forces, why should it matter what condition he is in?"

"You've got a jeep, Kevin," said a churchman up from Turramurra. "Which would you rather have it be, bumping along from Oenpelli or rusting in a heap at Pine Creek?"

"It's a lot better bumping along the dirt roads," rejoined the South Australian. "That's what it was made for!"

"Then," said the missionary, "why should it matter what condition the aborigines are in, if they lack any purpose for their own existence?"

"That's different," said Kevin. "A man can feel joy and sorrow, pleasure, and pain. He doesn't like to be made to do what he doesn't want to do."

"I agree entirely," said I. "But you are implying that all of us possess a moral obligation when you say that we ought to live for the good of humanity. If man is what you say, *ought* and *good* don't belong to the vocabulary, and there are no such things as moral obligation, moral value, free will, appreciation of beauty, and reason. Why should 'good' be rewarded and 'bad' punished?"

Relative Morality?

Attacks upon the idea of a moral Lawgiver have hurt the world. One reason for the increase of crime in modern society is undoubtedly the fact that young people are being taught that there is no absolute morality, that all morality is relative. As an illustration of relative morality, it may be pointed out that in certain states and countries, there is no speed limit on the open road; in others it is sixty-five miles or a hundred kilometers an hour; and in others it is much less than that. Each authority sets up the speed limit most suited to its own conditions of population and terrain.

So, say free-thinking philosophers, it is much the same regarding rules for human conduct: the authority in each society sets up the rules for that society. What is permitted in New Guinea may be forbidden in Canada. Of course, it is unwise to carry the illustration too far. Cannibalism is forbidden in Canada, but still persists in parts of Papua. To eat another human being is outrageous to a Canadian, but is acceptable to some Papuans and to some anthropologists, one of whom I heard defend the custom on the grounds that it helped meet the protein shortage. But what about the poor fellow who is being eaten: does not he have any rights, and are not those rights universal, not relative?

Universal Morality

Kant taught that the test of morality is in its universal application. In other words, if everyone behaved in this way, could life be maintained? If a big department store carried insurance against shoplifting, but everyone shoplifted, both department store and insurance company would go bankrupt.

Take, for example, the commandment: "Thou shalt not commit murder." Some societies seem less homicidal than others. Until Marcos as president called in unregistered guns, there were many times more murders per head of population in the Philippines than in the United States; and still many more murders per head of population occur in the United States than in the United Kingdom. The rate of killing in the urban guerrilla campaign in Northern Ireland is one-third that of Detroit, with the same population. Some may suggest that this supports the idea of relative morality, greater abhorrence of murder in some societies than others. But it seems obvious that in every society of the world everyone, everywhere, prefers not to be murdered.

Take the commandment: "Thou shalt not steal." In certain countries stealing is more common than in others. Is this entirely relative? One evening burglars broke into the expensive Los Angeles home of a man who was described as public enemy number one by the press. The so-called racketeer was indignant, saying: "What's the world coming to?"

And take the commandment: "Thou shalt not bear false witness." Even a child in school has realized that some people capable of telling lies without blinking an eyelid are themselves indignant when others try to deceive them. And so it goes. There seems to be a basic morality.

The Moral Argument for God

The moral argument can be stated in at least two ways. In mankind, there is an acute moral sense, unexplainable in the way one explains the senses of sight and hearing, therefore obviously implanted for our guidance by a higher Being. Or, since moral language makes sense, there must be some Source of all good and a Judge who arranges true justice.[2]

Immanuel Kant (who questioned the cosmological and the teleological arguments) insisted that the reality of God is a postulate of practical reason. It is morally necessary to assume the existence of God in order to sustain the concept of the best possible world, the greatest good for all, harmony with God's will being assurance of the greatest good.[3]

All thinking people are concerned with accounting for basic morality. Some objectors attribute moral sense to the training children receive throughout childhood, but cases are known where such training was lacking, yet individuals found a higher law at work through their consciences. And other objectors to the moral argument attribute moral sense to instinct, such as that of a bird in building a nest. But the instinct of the bird is adaptive or survival-oriented, and in moral sense there are multiplied instances which simply do not fit that category any more than that of training.

An objection to the more sophisticated argument from morality—that since moral language makes sense, there must be an objective Source—suggests that moral language could be objective and concern ideals that are not in fact realized anywhere. For example, no one can draw perfect circles, but we can still try and evaluate the attempt. But this does not prove the nonexistence of the Lawgiver.[4]

Presenting a Proper Hypothesis

Like the other proofs, the anthropological argument is bound to fail as a step-by-step demonstration of logical entailment. The argument is persuasive, not demonstrative. Atheists often grant the objectivity of a moral order which lays restraint upon humanity—what Immanuel Kant called the categorical imperative. It is possible, as at critical points in cosmology and teleology, for them to stop there. But if they are willing to consider the God of revelation as a serious hypothesis, they find themselves unable to nullify its validity.[5] The great difference between consideration of cosmology and teleology, on the one hand, and anthropology on the other is that the former involve external observation while the latter involves inside information—we do not just observe men: we are men. The moral order exists only in minds, and can it be derived from a mindless entity? The argument from the imperative of moral conduct is still best answered by the postulate of an Imperator, who has revealed Himself to us as Creator and Sustainer also.

CHAPTER SEVEN

Argument and Its Limits

From the foregoing, the strengths and weaknesses of the classic arguments can be briefly assessed. The cosmological argument provides a most satisfactory hypothesis to fit the facts of the beginning of the universe as generally held by scientists. It is compatible with all the evidence available, and its alternatives have produced no evidence at all. Yet it does not disprove the alternatives that claim that the universe has always existed in some form. The teleological argument provides a most satisfactory hypothesis to explain the apparently purposeful design in the universe. It too is compatible with all the evidence available, its alternatives being uncongenial to common sense. Yet it does not disprove the contention that some force less than God is responsible for the order in the universe. The anthropological argument likewise provides a most satisfactory hypothesis to explain the moral consciousness in man that is compatible with all the evidence. Its alternatives are less convincing, and they leave unanswered the question of the source of morality.

In logical entailment, it is possible to discredit argument after argument and so dismiss the case as unproven, not untrue. In presenting hypotheses, however, which seem to be compatible with the evidence, a series is encouraging to one who possesses a historical revelation of truth.

"What are you making?" I asked a man working wood.

"Something to sit on," he replied.

"Those look like stool legs," I commented, adding quite facetiously, "Are you going to sit on the points of three legs?"

"Don't be silly," he retorted. "These legs will firmly fit into the seat. I am going to sit on a comfortable seat."

The seat on which the Christian sits is the revelation of the Supreme Being. The legs supporting it are arguments that show that faith in God is not at all uncongenial to reason. The fact that some present an alternative account requiring no Creator or Designer or Imperator is not a refutation of the three hypotheses unless the alternative is shown to be a vastly superior hypothesis—which is not the case.

The Ontological Argument

The argument for God considered most obtuse by some but fascinating by others is the ontological argument, first stated by Anselm, Archbishop of Canterbury at the turn of the twelfth century.[1] It is the only argument logically prior to and independent of experience —the cosmological, and teleological, and anthropological arguments being posterior.

Anselm's argument was based on a definition that God is "something than which nothing greater can be conceived," therefore God is the most perfect entity; but an entity would be less than perfect if it did not exist; therefore God exists. Could such an argument be used to prove almost anything?

Aquinas rejected the Anselmic argument on the grounds that, because God's essence is unknown to us, the proposition of God's existence needs to be demonstrated by things that are better known to us—His effects; that it cannot be argued that what the definition of God proposes exists in fact unless and until it is admitted that the most perfect entity exists, which is denied by unbelievers.[2]

In the early seventeenth century, René Descartes newly formulated the ontological argument, also used by Leibniz. Immanuel Kant propounded a refutation of the Cartesian argument,[3] saying that an idea in the mind does not become any greater as an idea just because something corresponding to it exists outside the mind—the idea of a hundred dollar bill in the mind does not become an idea of more than that just because there is one in the bank teller's till. He stated that existence is not a predicate—that which is affirmed or denied about the subject of a proposition—which idea was expanded by Bertrand Russell in more recent days. And yet the ontological argument resurfaced in the writings of modern theologians and philosophers, such as Karl Barth and Charles Hartshorne. It is the argument least susceptible to illustration. It is the argument with least appeal to the layman.

To some people, the ontological argument seemed just too clever to be true. To others, it appeared to be inspired by a very profound truth. Anselm struck a sympathetic chord in the Christian heart by pointing out that he was not trying to call on reason to discover faith, but rather to understand faith. "I do not seek to understand in order to believe," he said, "but I believe in order to understand." And he made a good point there.

Pascal's Wager

There is an argument for God associated with the name of Blaise Pascal, the eminent French scientist of the mid-seventeenth century. Pascal's wager may be stated in the following terms: If a man believes in God, and God in fact exists, he will be rewarded; if he is mistaken, and God does not exist, he is none the worse. If a man disbelieves in God, and God in fact exists, he will suffer loss; if he is not mistaken, and God does not exist, he is none the better. Thus it is well worth while to believe, for the only possible gain is by believing, the most likely loss by not believing.[4]

Pascal's wager has been shouted down by critics. One has said that God is no fool, therefore if one's reasons for believing are just the gains he gambles on, God undoubtedly will see him for the hypocrite he is and deny him a reward; on the other hand, if a man has honest doubts, God surely will appreciate his doubts and reward him accordingly.[5]

A fairminded Christian would undoubtedly agree that the one who simply gambled on the gains expected from believing in God is likely to be disappointed. An informed Christian would point out that life eternal is not the automatic reward of those who agree that God exists, but is the gift of God to those who put their trust in Him through Jesus Christ.

Pascal's wager possesses certain merit. It should be stated in clearer terms: If believing is involved in the only possible gain, and disbelieving involved in the most likely loss, it is certainly well worthwhile to consider the claim of God on human lives, as this may lead to putting trust in Him for salvation from sin and eternal life.

The Argument from Values

A lifelong Oxford friend of mind, a retired principal of a famous college, was engaged in dialogue along with others with a team of Marxists from the Communist countries.[6]

"Of course, we appreciate art," they insisted, "but not in the fashion of the decadent West."

"When you look at a painting by a master," said my friend, pursuing the question, "do you seek to understand what sort of message the painter is seeking to convey?"

"Most certainly," replied a Communist. "That is why we so little appreciate a painting that seems to say nothing."

"Well, then," continued the Englishman, "do you ever look at a great work of nature and ask yourselves just what it is seeking to convey?"

This also is a persuasive hypothesis, not a logical proof.

Philosophy and Scripture

The arguments for the existence of God can be traced back to Plato. Do they then belong to Greek philosophy, not Judeo-Christian religion? Certainly, in the Old Testament, the existence of the Deity was not in question—the problem lay in competition of other gods for rightful worship.[7] The Psalmist in saying "The fool has said in his heart, there is no God!" was not protesting a denial of God's existence but of His power and wisdom and presence.[8] To establish the idea of Deity by means of argument was unknown among the prophets, and unnecessary in their times.

The Lord Jesus rebuked the world for not believing in God, but it seems clear that those who merited His rebuke for unbelief did not so much doubt His existence as live as if He did not exist. Theirs was a deficient faith.

In the Epistles, the unbelief of the world is often cited, but again it is not so much the hint of atheism as a protest against mere mental assent. The eleventh chapter of the Epistle to the Hebrews comes closest to modern apologetics in declaring that "he who comes to God must believe that He is, and that He rewards those who diligently seek Him." The Apostle James insisted that the devils also believe in God, yet tremble.[9] And the Apostle Paul insisted that ever since the creation of the world, God's unseen attributes have been plainly seen—His eternal power and divinity—in the things that He created.[10] Aquinas accepted this as an argument from design, but modern commentators usually treat it as creation revealing certain aspects of His nature.

It was Ambrose of Milan who said: "It has not pleased God to save His people with arguments." The truth of this, that salvation does not lie in mere assent to propositions, is obvious to all. But it must be realized that many young believers have lost their faith through arguments, and that many others doubting Christian truth have been moved to listen once again by arguments.

CHAPTER EIGHT

Counterargument

When my children were young, my daughter and son used to argue after the fashion of teenagers.

"I tell you, it is," said my daughter.

"I tell you, it is not," replied my son.

"But it is," insisted my daughter.

"But it is not," retorted my son.

"You know nothing," protested my daughter.

"You know nothing," mimicked my son.

"Oh, shut up," said my daughter.

"You shut up," answered my son.

"Both of you, shut up," said I, finally.

Dialogue is fruitful only when both debaters sincerely seek the truth and find a basis for discussion. It is fruitless always when one party or the other attempts to foreclose discussion by arbitrarily adopting debatable dicta.

Empirically Verifiable?

Bertrand Russell played a game of making rules which incapacitated his opponents in discussion of the issues. A similar development has been the proposition that nothing is really true—apart from a tautology, or definition which asserts nothing about reality—unless it can be empirically verified,[1] which notion narrows reality to a thing which may be demonstrated as true only by the five senses.

A Christian apologist, Thomas Corbishley, slyly asked an Oxford logical positivist:[2]

"Mr. Quinton, do you believe the statement that no statement is true unless it is verifiable?"

"Certainly!" replied Anthony Quinton.

"How can you verify that statement?"

"I cannot," was the reply.

"Then why do you believe it to be true?"

"I believe it to be true," insisted Quinton, "because it is true!"

"I believe God exists," retorted Corbishley, "because He does exist. Now where are we?"

In fairness, other secular philosophers have pointed out that religious statements are not the only statements which are unverifiable by empirical methods: moral statements fall into the same category. So kindly words have been said about the nobility of adopting Christianity as a way of life.

I am reminded of a symposium arranged by Dr. Howard Guinness in Oxford in which Sir David Ross made a stirring presentation of the idea that Christianity had not been tried and found wanting; it simply had not been tried.[3]

C. S. Lewis arose, and gently chided the higher-ranking academician, saying that he had "missed the boat": that the issue was not whether Christianity made people nicer, as faith in Santa Claus made small boys, but whether or not it was true, whether Christ died and rose again.

God—A Projection of Man's Mind?

The German, Ludwig Feuerbach, was possibly the most profound of all the atheists philosophizing in the nineteenth century. George Eliot, the woman novelist, translated into English his weighty German work in 1851, a decade after it was published. Feuerbach attempted to propound the notion that the whole idea of Almighty God was nothing more than a mere projection of man's magnified conception of himself imposed upon the universe.[4] This argument presented no proof at all, and seemed just wishful thinking.

I had reported for duty September 1944 on the island of Morotai, then the farthest advanced air base in the Pacific. My tentmate and I kept our minds off the air raids at night by discussing in a foxhole the problems of politics, science, philosophy, and religion. One midnight, the doctor said:

"Now listen, Chaplain. God is nothing more than an idea in people's minds. If you were to talk to a Solomon Islander and ask him about God, he thinks the thunder is God. But go to India and talk to an Indian peasant— he can explain the thunder, yet when an epidemic breaks out, he blames it on God and rushes to burn incense in his temple. Travel down to Australia and you find the educated Australian who explains both thunder and epidemics, yet uses God to cover up what he cannot understand. The farther you push back the frontiers of knowledge, the less you need an idea of God."

"You mean," said I, "that if the whole human race were destroyed in a catastrophe, God would cease to exist? Does not that leave unanswered questions about nature's order?

"Suppose you ask a primitive Papuan, 'Have you ever heard of King George?' And he replies, 'Yes, me British subject, belong King George.' But you say, 'How do you know there is such a person? Have you ever seen King George?' He replies, 'No, but me belong King George.'

"Then you say: 'What do you think King George is like?' The chief of a village may have four wives, the chief of a valley forty wives. The islander suggests that King George is a very big chief with four thousand wives!

"Travel from the Southwest Pacific to India and ask an Indian peasant whether he has ever seen King George, and what he is like. He thinks in terms of a local rajah, or of a maharajah nearby, or of the Mogul emperors, so he says that King George is the emperor of India.

"An Australian says: 'You Yanks don't understand at all. The King doesn't rule us, he reigns. He is a symbol.'

"Then you go to London and meet someone who says that he attended Cambridge University with King George, then a young prince. He recalls the king as an undergraduate.

"At a court function in London, you are glad to meet the Princess Elizabeth, who talks of her royal father as Daddy. You talk to Queen Elizabeth, who speaks of her husband.

"You talk next to an American tourist, who tells you that 'It's all right for the limeys to have a king, but we don't need one in America.'

"Then, finally, you talk to a Russian who describes King George as a 'catspaw of the capitalist system,' so that the Communists must destroy the monarchy in Britain as in Russia—that is his opinion.

"Seven different ideas of King George! But the most important thing to remember is that, if there is such a person as King George, seven different ideas do not change his character.

"Hence, throughout the world of humanity, there may be a thousand and one ideas of God, but, if there is a God, these ideas do not change His character."

There was a long silence before the all-clear sounded. We clambered out of the foxhole.

"Then," said my friend, the doctor, "How is anyone to know anything at all about God?"

"We only know as much as He chooses to disclose. We believe that He has chosen to present Jesus Christ as the living photograph of God."

The Myth of Santa Claus

My conversation with the pilot about atheism has been told. Another eager pilot dropped into my office for debate, and opened the conversation thus:

"Chaplain, were you talking to Lieutenant Petersen about how much do you know, and all that?"

I agreed, wondering what was to follow.

"Well, Chaplain," he went on, "could I ask you how much do you know?"

"Put me down for less than 1 percent also," said I.

"Very well, Chaplain. Then could I ask you if it is at all possible that Santa Claus could exist outside your 1 percent of knowledge?"

I saw that I had been trapped. Mercifully, the telephone rang, calling me to an emergency at the hospital.

"Can you see me at this time tomorrow?" I suggested.

"Nope," said the pilot. "I'm flying tomorrow. But I'll see you the day after next."

When he returned, I had a few questions to ask him.

"What is your definition of Santa Claus?"

"You know," he replied.

"Supposing I don't know?"

Further questions about Santa Claus followed.

"Is Santa Claus a little thin man?" I asked.

"No, he's a big fat man," he replied.

"Is he clean-shaven?"

"No, he has a white beard, white mustache, white hair."

"Does he wear a navy-blue suit?"

"No, he wears a red suit, with white fur trimming," he replied. Then he cut the questions short.

"You know and I know," he said, "that Santa Claus lives at the North Pole, and that he drives a reindeer team over the housetops, and comes down the chimney and fills the kids' stockings with toys. Okay?"

"Lieutenant," said I, "I'll give you a hundred and one scientific reasons for not believing in Santa Claus. First, he is too fat to come down any chimney. Second, to drive a reindeer team over the housetops is as difficult as to ride a bicycle to the moon. It is difficult to gain sufficient velocity. Santa Claus does not live at the North Pole.

"But what is your definition of God?" I went on. He did not reply, so I obliged him with one.

"God is the only infinite, eternal, and unchangeable Spirit, the perfect Being in Whom all things begin, continue and end. There is no scientific argument against that!" I added.

Prof. Michael Scriven, from whom I learned more in one hour than in a course in philosophy, erred, however, by offering the patent implausibility of the Santa Claus myth to illustrate the improbability of God's existence. I heard him state that intelligent adults no long- believed in God for the same reason that intelligent adults no longer believed in Santa Claus: Why do they no longer believe in Santa Claus? They can explain the pheomena for which his existence was invoked.[5] Why do atheists no longer believe in God? Because they can explain all the phenomena for which His existence was invoked? Emphatically, no! Many intelligent adults still affirm the existence of God, which cannot be said of Santa Claus. But Dr. Scriven maintained that nobody has given a disproof of the existence of Santa Claus, which is pure sophistry. To make the myth of Santa Claus of equal weight and value as the belief in a Supreme Being is an affront to intelligence and a damper on debate, closing down discussion.

Verification and Falsification

Prof. A. J. Ayer's logical positivism has declared that all theological utterances are meaningless, and Prof. Antony Flew has carried it further with the proposition that, not only are theological utterances without meaning, but that nothing could occur and nothing has occurred to disprove the conclusions of sophisticated theologians.[6]

There is a measure of truth in this observation. The fulminations of atheists little disturb believers who have enjoyed a vital experience with God. The problem of evil has less effect on those who have experienced the goodness of God. The fact remains that true believers derive their religious faith not from philosophy, but historic revelation.

But there is a strange neglect on the part of philosophers of Christianity as recorded history, rather than as a philosophy. The New Testament is better attested today as history than ever before, and the story of the Resurrection stands unchallenged as recorded history. "Schonfield's Plot" which seems to discredit the Resurrection story has had short shrift with historians, if not with journalists.[7]

The Invisible Gardener

Antony Flew adapted a tale told by Prof. John Wisdom to present a modern criticism of the teleological argument in a story of two explorers who stumbled upon a clearing in the jungle in which were growing flowers and weeds. One explorer insists that some gardener must tend the plot; the other refuses to believe it. They pitch their tents and set a watch. No gardener is ever seen. In case the gardener is invisible, they electrify a barbed-wire fence and patrol it with a bloodhound, but no gardener is ever discovered. The believing explorer still insists that an invisible, intangible, insensible, and elusive gardener visits the plot secretly, and the skeptic asks, "How does an invisible, intangible, eternally elusive gardener differ from an imaginary gardener or no gardener at all?"[8]

The invisible gardener hypothesis falls far short of the versatility of that of the watchmaker, and it deals with a teleological proof rather than a teleological hypothesis. Its weakness lies in the same area as that of my professor at Northwestern University who insisted that God must be verified within the circle of scientific knowledge.

The believing explorer in Professor Flew's story appears so stupid that it is hard to believe that he even managed to get as far as Manaus on the Amazon in a river steamer. All the gardeners of Brazilian and British experience have handled visible and tangible things with visible and tangible hands. To depict an invisible God as an invisible gardener requires not a parable (which is a plausible story) but a fairy tale. This fairy tale itself assumes that God, the reality behind all objects perceived by the senses and the originator of matter, is material—to be verified by electric fences and bloodhounds. As Rheinallt Williams pointed out, belief in an invisible power that accounts for the visible world is not patently absurd (as was the invisible gardener) but has made sense to the brightest minds in the history of thought as well as to common sense. Multitudes of capable people have concluded that the world is dependent on something other than itself for its existence.[9] Even an ardent atheist could concede that, upon first sight, belief in the existence of God is the most plausible explanation of the cosmos. Furthermore, God is not eternally elusive, for He has disclosed Himself in well-attested revelation and there are millions who seriously claim experience of Him.

Faith is a Choice

Essentially, the Christian gains his faith in God from historic revelation, not from philosophic speculation. This written revelation is not the vague experience of individuals of more or less or no reliability, but the authenticated record of God Almighty's intercourse with men as found in Sacred Scripture, subjected to the scrutiny of centuries.

I have had occasion to refer to Dr. Gerhard Dirks, an expert in the computer field. He had told me that he had worked in Germany's most advanced scientific research complex. Whatever faith he had, he had lost.

After the conclusion of hostilities, he came to the United States. I asked him how he had found his faith again. As I recall it, the conversation went like this.

"Orr," he asked, "what do you know about automation?"

"Just a layman's knowledge. My wife uses a dishwashing machine. She can tell you when it is rinsing and when it is sudsing. I was more curious, so I opened it up to see what made it so behave, and I found a steel disc with a code cut in its teeth. That's automation, isn't it?" I asked.

"You understand," said the expert, "that the code needed to be built into it?"

Then he went on to describe more complicated things.

"Suppose you wanted to build an automated plow," he suggested. "You would need a little gasoline motor for the power. You would need a clutch; and a blade that could be raised and lowered. You would need some direction-finding equipment. And so, you could design a plow that could plow a furrow across the field.

"But," he went on, "it's not much good if you have to send a man after it to turn it around. So you add a turning device. That means that you must add to it some further bits of information, as we call them. You understand?

"Now you've got a plow that's plowing furrows back and forth across the field. It hits a rock. So now you must design a rock-ejector. This must stop the machine, throw the motor into neutral, lift the blade, eject the rock, lower the blade, move into gear, and go on plowing.

"Now the plow is running back and forth across the field, but it hits a root. You can't eject a root, so you must design a root-cutter. All that takes a little more information, so bits of information are added.

"Then the plow hits a corner of the field that's flooded, though it's not always flooded. So you arrange for it to stop at the edge of the water and send a signal to headquarters; then you tell it to back away and start another furrow. That means, if you have followed me, that the more complicated the machine, the more bits of information you must put into it at the beginning. Do you follow me?"

So far, I had followed him.

"Let me go on with my illustration," continued Dr. Dirks. "It is possible to build a computer to play chess. But it is not an economic project. A seventeen-year-old boy can be taught to play chess much more economically. How many bits of information are required for such a computer? How many bits of information for the human brain?

"The most complicated machine that we have," explained the expert, "is the human being. The human brain can play chess. So I began to try to work out the mathematical probability, that is, the number of bits of information, to account for the human brain."

We discussed the fact that to build a machine capable of building another machine exactly like itself— reaching into a bin and taking a screw here, another there, a piece of wire here, a bolt there and so forth— would require bits of information equal to two to the fifteen-hundredth power, a staggering figure, as any mathematician knows.[10]

And likewise, at the point of human conception, a single little cell receives instruction through the DNA genetic code to divide in two; to divide into four; into eight; and into sixteen; until it becomes a mass of cells.

Then the specialization sets in; some cells are told to become as hard as wood—they become bone—and others are told to lengthen out to become nerves. Others are told to cluster together and form a television camera and convey visual impressions to the brain. Others become the brain and store up memory and the like.

"Orr," said Dr. Dirks, "I tried to work it out.[11] It's just fantastic. Somebody still could say that all of it is possible without a plan—yes, it's still remotely possible. I decided to choose for myself. And I believe the only way to explain it all is to attribute it to divine Intelligence."

Not only did Gerhard Dirks find the answer to many a scientific question, but he found the answer to many personal problems as well. He soon allied himself with the Christian Business Men's Committee and shared his testimony.

CHAPTER NINE

The Problem of Evil

After braving Santa Claus and the invisible gardener as well as Feuerbach, it is almost with relief to meet another argument, a straight denial of God on the ground of ever-present evil, one that makes the Christian scholar wince.

The problem of evil is one of the most crucial protests raised by unbelievers against the fact of God. Believers may insist that countless experiences simply make no sense apart from God's existence; likewise unbelievers may protest that specified experiences make no sense if God exists.

The Inconsistent Triad?

The skeptic, David Hume, presented three points:[1] the world manifests instances of suffering: God is supposedly omnipotent, omniscient, and omnipresent; and God is wholly good; but these three propositions cannot be held together. Any two would contradict the third.[2]

If God is wholly good, and God is omnipotent, omniscient, and omnipresent, why would He permit such suffering? If God is good, and there is evil, then He cannot be omnipotent! If He is omnipotent, and there is evil, then He cannot be good! Therefore, as it is obvious that there is suffering in the world, God cannot xist. According to Hume, this conclusion is "so short," so clear," and "so decisive." It has enjoyed a continu-g popularity with atheists and skeptics.

There are two kinds of evil—natural evil and moral vil. A wayfarer takes shelter under a great rock which, oosened by the rain, comes tumbling down, killing im. That is natural evil. A wayfarer takes shelter in a ttle hut, but a wicked robber stabs him to death. That moral evil.

Natural Evil

What would be the alternative to those natural laws 1at sometimes cause human suffering? If it were pos-ble to suspend the law of gravity to prevent some eople from being crushed by rocks, what would be the ffect upon the rest of the solar system? It would fly part with disastrous results for all living things on arth.[3]

But could not Almighty God prevent disasters, say, y appointing angels to watch over wayfarers sheltering nder rocks? Carried to its logical conclusion, the idea staggering. Winter snow would be banned because of ccasional hazard to human life; spring rains would be arred because of occasional inconvenience of floods. ar better to make the best of possible worlds, the cological ideal, avoiding concentration of population 1 areas subject to flood and not building dwellings over arthquake faults. By all means, let us try to prevent pidemics. Let us heal the sick and ease the pain. :hallenge is needed for social well-being.

It must never be forgotten that killing[4]—the most icious crime of humans—is something that nature

imposes upon every living thing once. Death is inevita
ble. Yet it is a great world in which we live, so much
for which to be thankful.

Moral Evil

By far, the greater part of human misery is caused by
man's inhumanity to man, and not by the hazards of
nature. But what about this moral evil? Well do I remember an air raid on the island of Morotai, when a
direct hit demolished the post office hut, killing the
sorters. It was saddening to watch the troops place the
bodies of their comrades on a truck, to be shipped
away for burial. A soldier said to me, bitterly: "If there
is a God, why does He allow this sort of thing?" I
replied, "We are both upset. See me tomorrow."

"If you were God," said I, "how would you prevent
this?"

"I would make people," he replied, "incapable of
fighting and killing and making war."

"In other words," I commented, "automatic machines?"

At Oxford, I met a Royal Navy officer who disap-
proved of the conduct of American troops in Britain,
saying that they were overdressed, overpaid, and over-
sexed, something that could have been said of British
tommies in Egypt also, or soldiers anywhere away from
home.

"I served," said I, "on an island on the equator
where three thousand American troops were stationed,
and in six whole months, there was not one instance of
even a stolen kiss."

"I can't believe it," he replied.

I insisted that it was so, but honesty compelled me to

add that there was not a solitary woman on the island. There was no virtue in doing good in the absence of some opportunity of doing wrong.

A couple known to friends of mine had a son who was studying in a college a thousand miles away from home. The parents knew that their son had taken a fancy to a girl whose own parents had informed them of her coquettish propensities. They hoped against hope that the infatuated youth would discover his mistake in time, and terminate the friendship. Meanwhile, the student's class records—once first-rate—were suffering, until at last he left the college and returned home discouraged.

One day, the son received a letter from the girl, a letter so upsetting that the parents judged its contents to contain the tantalizing news of yet another love affair, an ending of whatever understanding there had been. They shared his misery, hoping for the best. The mother later phoned her husband in distress to warn him that his son had taken off impetuously in his father's car for the distant college town. They waited patiently at home, hoping that the telephone would ring, not with the news of a highway crash but of his second thoughts about the purpose of the journey. At last, the father contacted the police who simply said: "Yes, we can stop him on the way. But you must first charge him with the misappropriation of your car."

The parents talked it over, but decided not to do it that way. Much as they wanted to stop the runaway, they would not shame their son, nor hurt his self-esteem, even though he clearly was at fault. They could have stopped him in his tracks, but much preferred to let him learn his lesson as a man. At last, he called them from a point four hundred miles away, and the father flew to join him on the journey back. Alas, it would be nice to tell a happy ending to the story, but the foolish fellow tried to reinstate the affair, and suffered even more before he learned his lesson.

God can create free creatures, but cannot force them to do good, or they would not be free.[5] He cannot prohibit free creatures from doing evil, and some so do; that this happens does not tell against God's goodness or His omnipotence.

A More Consistent Tetrad?

"But then is God omnipotent?" Scripture reveals Him as such, but the context qualifies the claim. "Could God create a rock so big that He could not lift?" God is not foolish. The omnipotence of God is intrinsic: God cannot lie, for example. God can do anything that is in keeping with His character. He cannot fake free will for man.

Hume's propositions need to be restated.[6] God is wholly good; God is omnipotent in keeping with His character; and there is suffering in the world, due to evil; but there are morally sufficient reasons for such suffering and evil. In this statement, evil is an inevitable consequence of being, natural as well as moral; but moral evil involves intelligent choice of wrong instead of right, therefore man is culpable.

Lest academic discussion of the problem of evil should sound like a lack of compassion for the world's misery, it must be added that, while the revelation of God withholds from the believer a full comprehension of the mystery of suffering, giving only a cryptic hint of its very origin, the Christian message is very explicit in telling the believer what to do to relieve the suffering.

How true it is that many claiming the name of Christian have added to the world's great suffering by their cruelties and intolerance.[7] These they did not get from the message of Christ, and they denied Him in so behaving. But it can also be said that those believers who delight to do the will of God have been the greatest exemplars of compassion, initiating so many noble projects for the amelioration of suffering as well as sharing in the creation of a public conscience against social evil.

A famous scientist and I sat down at a table to discuss a problem in probability, and a stranger joined us, saying that he wanted to ask a question as soon as we were free. "If there is a God," he protested, "why is He so cruel?"

He had serious difficulty with the problem of deformity in children, of suffering in sickness. Said I:

"If someone walked by, and my friend and I greeted him cordially, but you turned away, I would ask you why? And if you insisted, 'I detest him because he is so cruel!' I would ask you if you knew him. If you said no, I would tell you that everyone I knew who knew him thought that he was wonderfully kind.

"Why don't you check with those who know God?"

This man, an airlines executive, professed conversion that night.

CHAPTER TEN

Faith and Experience

The sun was dropping rapidly into the glassy waters of the western Pacific, the multipasteled sky with its huge pink-and-gray-and-white thunderheads reflected in the placid ocean mirror. A group of us airmen were sitting on a log stranded on the beach of an island north of New Guinea's western peninsula, the Vogelkop.

"Chaplain," said a sergeant, "you religious guys bother me. A mathematician can take you to the blackboard, and an astronomer to the telescope, but all you religious guys do is to talk about faith."

"I wish," I replied, "I could oblige you with some kind of scientific test of the fact of God. But, of necessity, there is none. Neither telescope nor microscope nor litmus paper nor Geiger counter will suffice. But," I went on, "faith is a kind of insight."

"I don't get it," he protested. "Faith is just superstition. And with educated people, it is a refined superstition."

"No, no," I answered. "Faith is not at all superstition. Superstition is contrary to reason. Faith is agreeable to reason. There is that difference."

The sergeant still looked baffled. He did not understand. So I suggested an experiment for illustration.

"I would like to ask you men to cooperate with me in an illustration. Let us pretend that this is a class of students blind from birth, and I have been asked to give a lecture on the beauty of the spectrum."

They entered into the spirit of the situation. I began by saying briskly to the class:

"Gentlemen, I am aware of your handicap so, if I go too fast for you, raise your hand and ask me any question to help your understanding of my statements.

"Gentlemen, the spectrum in its beauty is a manifestation of light—"

Immediately, a hand was raised and a voice protested:

"Tell us, what is light?"

"That's a good question," I commented. "Light is a radiation—"

"Like what?"

"Light is part of the spectrum of energy," I explained, thinking quickly to put myself into blind eyes. "You know what heat is? Just as heat radiates warmth, light makes things visible."

Twenty to one gave them an unfair advantage. Another hand was raised, with another question:

"What is the meaning of *visible*?"

"*Visible*," I replied, "is a word derived from the French. It means 'able to be seen.'"

"Sorry, sir," he retorted. "We don't understand you. We have never seen anything, whatever that means."

I smiled. They were making my point very quickly.

"Let me go on with my lecture," I asked. "If you let a beam of light from the window strike a prism of glass, it will break up into a spectrum on the wall, like a rainbow."

"What is a rainbow?" was the next question.

"Come on, now," I protested. "You have all heard

about a rainbow. A rainbow is caused by the refraction of the sun's rays in a rain cloud. It is red and blue and green . . ."

"Sir," observed another participant, "none of us have ever seen a rainbow. Would you mind telling us what is red and blue and green?"

"Red—everyone's blood is red. Blue—the sky is blue. Green—the grass is green."

But we all realized that blind persons have no idea of the redness of blood, the blueness of the sky, or the greenness of the grass. My hecklers had not given up yet.

"What is the characteristic of blue?" asked one.

"Its blueness, I suppose," I replied amid laughter.

Then a technical sergeant raised his hand.

"Sir, is it possible to describe the range of the spectrum in scientific language without referring to the kind of feeling that you call sight?"

"You are quite right," I replied. "Just as a nerve in one's leg conveys a sensation of pain to the brain, so an optic nerve conveys the different sensations of red and blue and green. It is a feeling."

"Then could you describe red and blue in scientific terms without referring to this feeling that none of us have?"

"There was a Swedish scientist named Angström," I said, "who measured the wave lengths of the spectrum. Red is 7000 angströms, blue is 4800 angströms."

I waited until this would sink into their minds, and to give them enough time to assess its impact on the blind.

"Now," I asked, "would all blind students nod their heads and say, 'Thank you very much, sir. Now we understand. And we do not need to depend upon mere feeling. We have a scientific definition.' "

Rejecting the Evidence

All analogies fall short at certain points. It has been objected that, while a blind man cannot argue that there is no such sense as sight because he lacks it, he may confirm the sense of sight by referring to some other sense. He cannot see a chair in the middle of the room, but he can feel it when he falls over it.[1] So the blind man may infer that his friend who claims to have sight has access to a kind of knowledge that he himself does not have.

The modern atheist insists that there is no way by which one may distinguish a man who claims to have a religious sense and is correct from one who is mistaken. In this, he is both wrong and right. The believer's faith may be distinguished from superstition, which is contrary to reason. Furthermore, I have met believers who formerly were unbelievers, and every last one insisted that he had evidence of God in his life.

The believer's faith may be supported by the good effects thereof upon his own life. The believer's faith may be confirmed to himself by answers to prayer, though the skeptic disregards the evidence and claims that he was only lucky. Occasionally, the believer's faith is strengthened by some such providence as healing, but the skeptic nullifies the evidence by saying that the healing was psychosomatic! But it is rather odd to claim that X rays offered by an expert showing that a bone had lengthened seven millimeters after prayer confirms the notion that the healing was accomplished only in the mind.[2]

Is there some perceptual awareness of God? Of course there is. The testimony to this fact is given by a myriad of witnesses who claim to be more sure of this than of their own well-being.

Instead of being thus compelled by force of logic to believe in God, we find ourselves persuaded to respond to Him with "all our hearts and souls and minds and strength" accepting freely proffered love and moral claim in happy recognition of God as infinitely higher in wisdom and in power, yet our eternal Father. Faith is much more than a mere assent of the mind.

Faith is an insight, a perception, an awareness of truth beyond the confirmation—or even definition—of science.

So once again, the argument becomes a plea for a very persuasive hypothesis.[3] The believer simply says that faith is proved by general personal experience. But how is the believer to convince the atheist of this when the latter utterly refuses to experiment with faith, or tries to test it out facetiously?

The Foundation of Faith

It is not enough for keen believers to insist that faith in God inspires them to resolve their problems. The question always is, not "Does it work?" but "Is it true?" The Good News of Jesus Christ is substantiated good news.

Faith must have a firm foundation. The revelation of God is presented in the Old and New Testaments, the Old an unfolding revelation of God, the New unsurpassed. The Christian may begin by reference to the story of Jesus Christ, found in documents that are well attested by consensus of historians. The Gospels have the ring of truth. They not only tell the story of the Man who claimed to be the Deity in human form, but they tell of His atoning death and glorious resurrection from the dead.

In the message of the gospel, the first recorded word —in the mouth of John the Baptist, Jesus Christ, the twelve disciples, the Apostle Peter and Apostle Paul —is the word *repent*, not to feel remorse, but to change one's thinking. Regeneration follows such repentance and conversion.[4]

Those who testify that they have thus obeyed the message of repentance uniformly witness to its effects. I have known the humblest folk without an elementary education who have verified it for themselves, likewise scholars in the highest echelons of the academic world who testified the same, for they were born again of the Spirit of God.

In its last analysis, faith is a step, not so much a leap into the dark, but a confident step to a bright reality. Faith is the assurance of that for which we hope, the conviction of the reality of the unseen.

CHAPTER ELEVEN

Attested Revelation

The point was made earlier that the Christian faith does not depend upon philosophers for authenticity, but on truth revealed in events attested by eyewitnesses and conveyed by documents sustained by historical verification.

When Christians claim that their faith is based on divine revelation, they do not thereby mean that some folk are fortunate enough to have had the existence of God revealed to them. Rather they are speaking of a revelation once for all made and conveyed to succeeding generations.

A leading apologist for atheism once told me that every founder of a great religion claimed to be God! The names of the founders of Buddhism, Confucianism, Judaism, and Islam are recognized by most to have been Gautama, Kung-fu-tze, Moses, and Mohammed; Shinto and Hinduism lacking such authentic figures. If Gautama Buddha be considered an atheist, Confucius must be recognized as an agnostic, hence neither may be reckoned as a claimant for deity. Moses and Mohammed most modestly admitted no higher a status than that of prophet, so Jews and Muslims would indignantly deny any charge of deifying their leaders.

The Roman Emperors and those of Japan claimed to be divine, but only in the sense of demanding worship, not in claiming omnipotence or immortality. In recent times, an enterprising Afro-American named Father

Divine claimed deity, but the pretension has gone by default. More recently, the Guru Maharaj-ji has persuaded multitudes of gullible Westerners to contribute their dollars for his support as God, but the "Mother of God" has denied her son's claim.

Consequently, Christians claim seriously that God's revelation of Himself in Jesus Christ is unique. The fact that the Christian faith has survived the attrition of the centuries and has persuaded and is still persuading many of the best minds to accept its truth surely demands a fair consideration of its declarations.

The case for the acceptance of the New Testament as an attested historical document must be thoroughly examined.

How Old are the Manuscripts?

Everyone has heard the name of Julius Caesar and knows of his account of the Gallic Wars.[1] The reliability of his writings go unchallenged, yet is it commonly known that the earliest surviving manuscript dates from the tenth century, nearly a thousand years after its original draft was penned? The same is true of other ancient writers.

Nonetheless there are critics of the New Testament who complain that its earliest whole manuscripts date from 325 to 350 A.D. On Christmas Day, 1933—well do I remember—the British government and people bought from the USSR for a hundred thousand pounds the Codex Sinaiticus, containing all but a few verses of the New Testament and more than half of the Old Testament—paralleling the Codices Vaticanus and Alexandrinus.

I also remember twenty months later crossing the

Aegean Sea with a graduate from Harvard, who later became minister of a Unitarian church in Washington, D.C. With the advantage of a university education, he told me that the Gospel of John had been written in second half of the second century. All that I could say in my inexperience was that it seemed to describe the same Jesus as the other Gospels. Since that time, the John Ryland Library in the University of Manchester, England, has exhibited the oldest fragment of the New Testament, dating from 130 A.D., a portion of the Gospel of John copied within a generation of its publication, therefore confirming the traditional view of its composition before the end of the first century and denying the theory that it was written after the year 160 A.D.[2]

Sir Frederic Kenyon, director of the British Museum, declared emphatically that the books of the New Testament were written in the latter half of the first century, and that it has come down to us substantially as it was written, its authenticity and general integrity finally established. No other ancient book possesses anything like such early and plentiful testimony to its text, which is substantially sound in the judgment of every unbiased scholar.[3]

The Variant Readings

It has been noted that the average time span between the writing of ancient documents (such as Cæsar, Aristotle, Plato, and Herodotus) and the earliest surviving manuscripts exceeds a thousand years. In the case of the New Testament, the comparable time span is two hundred years, shortened by fragments going back to fifty years.

It is said that all of the New Testament has been quoted by the earliest Christian writers, except for a few verses. Ignatius, born A.D. 70 and martyred A.D. 110, quoted very extensively from a dozen or more of the New Testament books. So also did Polycarp of Smyrna, a disciple of John. And it may be added that every decade produces discoveries that strengthen the case for the integrity of the Scriptures rather than otherwise.

Other critics profess to be more disturbed by the fact that there are a hundred and fifty thousand variant readings of the New Testament. Of course, this figure is liable to be misunderstood, for if a single word is misspelled in one thousand manuscripts, this repeated error is counted as a thousand variant readings. Other such variants are minor changes in the order of words. Philip Schaff came to the conclusion that no more than four hundred of the variants raised any doubt, and only fifty of these were significant. Not one of the variants altered an article of faith or a precept of duty unsus tained by other passages.[4] The wealth of the attestation, declared F. F. Bruce, is so great that the true reading is almost invariably bound to be preserved by at least one of the thousands of witnesses.[5]

Authority in Scripture

In the early fifties, I was addressing a meeting of the students at California Institute of Technology, reputedly possessors of the highest IQs in North America. From the floor, a student asked:

"Is it not a fact that the New Testament as we have it today was put into its present form in the fourth century?"

"The canon was completed then," I replied.

"Is it not a fact that there was a Gospel of Peter and a Gospel of Thomas?"

"Yes, and the Shepherd of Hermas and the Teaching of the Twelve Apostles . . ."

"Why weren't they included in the canon?"

I explained that no one in the early days had ever heard of the pseudo-Gospels, hence they were later suspect.

"The Gospel of Thomas appeared to be a pious fraud. It told stories of the childhood of Jesus, molding clay pigeons and throwing them into the air to fly away."

The other two that I had mentioned were deemed genuine documents, but were not written by the Apostles or upon apostolic authority. They were invaluable, I explained, for their historical and doctrinal content as postapostolic data but were not included in the canon of apostolic writings.

"Is it not a fact," asked the student, "that the bishops and fathers of the Church thus decided what would go into the New Testament? And does not that mean that the authority rests in the Church and not in the Scriptures themselves?"

I could see an argument for oral tradition over written documents arising, but I told him to proceed.

"As I heard it," said the student with a smile, "there were a lot of scriptures floating around—some genuine, some otherwise. So the bishops and Fathers of the Church put the genuine and the disputed books on the floor and prayed over them, whereupon the genuine ones jumped by themselves onto the table."

We all laughed. It was not difficult to explain that, when the Synod of Hippo in A.D. 393 listed the twenty-seven books of the New Testament, it did not create any authority for them which they did not already possess. And the Synod of Carthage, four years later, likewise recognized the canon of the New Testament books previously established by the precedent of past generations of Christians.

Apocryphal Writings

Just as the New Testament writings were committed to the care of the Christian church, so the Old Testament was committed to the care of the people of Israel. From earliest times, the Hebrew Scriptures were divided into the Law, the Prophets, and the Writings. There was a unanimity of opinion among the Jews regarding the canonicity of the books now presented as the thirty-nine of the Old Testament, and an equally firm rejection of those of the Apocrypha—which abound in geographical and historical inaccuracies, teach doctrines and practices at variance with canonical scripture, and present legends, short novels, and the like as well as secular history. Christ and the Apostles quoted only the canonical Old Testament Scriptures.

CHAPTER TWELVE

Inspiration of Scripture

"I'll tell you what I believe. I believe that if you do your best, God will do the rest!" said a man to me.

"That's a nice religion," I replied. "But what is your authority for so believing?"

"That's what I believe!" responded he. And nothing I could say in any way dislodged him from the imperturbable finality of his conviction.

"Very well, then," said I. "If doing your best is all that is required for your salvation, do you always do your best?"

He admitted that he did not always do his best.

"Then," said I, "if the great requirement is that you must do your best, you are disqualified, according to you!"

What struck me as particularly odd was his supposition that all that mattered was his adherence to his notion, without authority of any kind, in reason or in revelation.

It ought to be taken for granted that, for the Christian, the supreme authority is Jesus Christ. If a man should call himself a Marxist, yet discredit the authority of Marx, without doubt, he ought to choose a fairer appellation for himself. The paramount authority for every Christian is Jesus Christ.

But all our knowledge of the Lord is found in Sacred Scriptures, for which authority is claimed. When Paul the Apostle wrote to Timothy, "All scripture is given by

the inspiration of God," the component parts of the
New Testament had not yet been written.[1] But, without
a doubt, his affirmation of inspiration was applied by
Christians to the New Testament as well as the Old.

Schools of Authority

How then is anyone to account for the various
schools among professing Christians in this field? It is
easy to conclude that Christians are by no means one in
mind or voice concerning this authority.

To generalize, the schools of thought thereon may be
divided into three: traditional, rational, and evangelical. There have been those whose chief reliance has
been upon tradition, not denying reason or discounting
revelation but subordinating them to the traditions of
the Church; there are those who discount revelation
and tradition in order to enthrone capricious human
reason. And there are those who recognize tradition
and defer to human reason, but insist that revelation is
decisive in themes involving God—this the evangelical
position, simply based upon Good News of Christ revealed in the Evangels.

Traditional

I was walking round a lovely garden in the palmy
state of Kerala in India, my host a priest of the Mar
Thoma Church. I noticed an unfamiliar tree, and asked
its name.

"That's a cashew-nut tree," he explained.

It was the first time I had noticed such a tree, so I
went across the lawn to inspect its leaves and fruit.

"What is this imposed upon the fruit?" I asked.

"That's the seed!" he replied.

"Up on top of the fruit? Outside?"

"Yes," he explained, agreeing that this arrangement was extremely rare in botany, tropical or temperate.

"It is supposed," said he, "among some Syrian believers that God did not create the cashew-nut tree. Moses did. You see, Moses went to the Lord and said: 'You've made everything. I would like to make something. I would like to make a tree.'

Permission granted, Moses reportedly worked for many a month in making a tree. Then he brought it to the Lord for inspection. The Lord congratulated him upon making a cashew-nut tree, but then he asked Moses where he had put the seed. Alas, Moses had forgotten the seed, so he placed the seed on top of the fruit, like a candle on a cake.

So much for a Malabar tradition. I liked the story so well that I have told it once a week for many years. But I do not seriously believe it, quite apart from a passing acquaintance with botany. I have read the five books of Moses and references to Moses in the Old Testament, allusions to Moses in the New Testament, quotations in the Talmud and expositions in the commentaries, but not a word regarding Moses making a cashew-nut tree.

But, I readily concede, this does not inflict an injury on anyone believing in the legend—providing it is never made a dogma of the Church. There are many innocent traditions in Christendom, the celebration of Christmas as the birthday of Jesus, for example, which is no more correct than the celebration of the British royal birthday in June.

"Unbaptized babies," I was told, "cannot go to heaven nor do they go to hell. They go to a place called limbo, where they are happy, but never see the face of God."

I asked for some authority for this notion, absent in both Scriptures and apostolic teaching, but was offered only oral tradition, not the written word. Other pious notions even further contradict the teaching of the Word, derived from philosophic speculation or scholastic rationalization based on faulty premises.

Rational

In a courtroom, a philosophical speculation or a scientific theory is of value, but not if it is in conflict with attested evidence of eyewitnesses properly scrutinized. Reason is of inestimable value in interpreting revealed truth, but it is not supreme—the revelation is.

This may best be illustrated in the Library of Congress in Washington, where lies the so-called Jefferson Bible—not really a Bible, but a selection of passages from the Gospels made by Thomas Jefferson, ardent patriot and zealous deist.[2] Jefferson did not believe in prayer, so the prayers were omitted; he did not believe in miracles, so the miracles were left out; he disputed Christ's claim to deity, so the pertinent passages were ignored. By what authority? Jefferson once protested that he was a Christian but only in the way that Jesus would have wanted anyone to be a Christian. He did not explain how he or anyone could learn what Jesus wanted, apart from the New Testament.

In nominal Christendom, the rationalists have every bit as numerous a following as the traditionalists. They used to be called modernists, but the designation is far from modern, as is their fallacy. Some call them liberals, and forget that *'liberal'* is properly an adjective to qualify a noun. They should not be called evangelicals, but rather Christohumanists, more humanist than Christian.

Evangelical

The evangelical position is simply stated. If anyone desires to know what Jesus Christ said or did, let him read the New Testament, the Gospel narratives being the authority for what is safely believed by Christians. Tradition may be helpful and reason desirable in the interpretation of the New Testament, but the authority rests in the written word. The Scripture itself claims inspiration by the Spirit of God, and the Lord Jesus promised the guidance of the Spirit into all truth.

The Doctrine of Inspiration

What do we mean by *inspiration*? Let us consider first what is not meant. In the original Greek, the word used means not inspired, but God-breathed. Therefore, it is not meant merely that the Scriptures are inspiring in any collective, subjective sense.

"I believe that the Scriptures are inspired," said a friend of mine, cheerfully, "because they inspire me."

That sort of thing could be said of Shakespeare, or any one of a hundred and one writers. Something more objective is meant than that.

On the other hand, I have met worthy people who seemed to think that God Almighty had secluded certain individuals, and dictated the Scriptures to them, word by word, sentence by sentence, paragraph by paragraph.

Scripture itself soon disposes of the idea of mechanical dictation. The Apostle Paul wrote to the Corinthians and deplored the party loyalties among them. Said he:[3]

"I thank God I baptized none of you" (that was his first recollection) "except Crispus and Gaius" (that was his first amendment) "lest any should say that I baptized in my own name" (that was his first explanation). "I also baptized the household of Stephanas" (that was his second amendment) "and if there be any others, I cannot remember" (that was his final comment). What was his point? He repudiated the idea that he had inaugurated a church party at Corinth. It is very difficult to sustain the idea that these words were dictated to him by the Holy Spirit, and very difficult not to say that the Apostle was using his memory, inspired by all means by the Spirit. The example by no means exhausts the arguments against mechanical dictation.

The text in the Second Letter to Timothy not only stresses the dynamic of inspiration of Scripture—God-breathed—but also the scope of it—"all scripture"[4]—which is plenary. In other words, no one is free to pick and choose which verses to accord dynamic inspiration, though he may interpret them in varied ways, according to common sense and context.

I was flying high above the dust in India once, when I discovered that my seat companion was a distinguished churchman whose theology, I guessed, was more "rational" and less "evangelical" than mine. Happily, we found a lot in common, then touched upon a difference.

"But, surely," he protested, "all of us are evangelical."

"In degree," I suggested, "according to our attitude

to the New Testament. For example, do you accept the clear account of the conception and birth of Jesus?"[5]

"Well," he replied. "Only two of the Evangelists make mention of those circumstances, so I hardly think that they are important. And the Apostle Paul made no reference at all, which is a very significant omission."

"There is no evidence in history," I replied, "that the Apostle Paul or any apostle, or any one of the early Church fathers, did not share the common belief of the early Church about the birth of Jesus. But do you really think that what the Apostle Paul wrote or omitted to write was significant?"

"Yes, indeed," he insisted.

"Well, then. Do you agree that the Apostle Paul clearly taught the doctrine of the Second Coming of Christ? You do! And do you believe in the Second Coming?"[6]

Alas, this was not one of his preferred doctrines either. He was not much better than Thomas Jefferson in this regard, but we parted cordially at the Nagpur airport.

Human—and Divine

While believing that the Scriptures are dynamically and plenarily inspired, their content divine, it must be quickly recognized that they are human literature, the word of man as well as the Word of God. In literature are found modes (history, narrative, poetry, and proverbs) and devices (style, figures of speech, symbols and allegory); in Sacred Scripture these are likewise found. One must learn to distinguish modes and devices, not treating poetry as history nor confusing allegory with narrative.

The best known psalm is a poem.[7] It was written by a poet who spent his boyhood watching sheep, and it places a believer in the circumstances of a sheep. Who would want to take it literally? Most people would prefer to lie down in a comfortable bed indoors than in green pastures. But, taken as a poem, it tenders peerless beauty and profounder comfort. In the Book of the Judges, Jotham told the men of Shechem how the trees of the field arranged an election of one of their number to be king.[8] Does anyone believe that the vine refused to leave its grapes to be promoted to the monarchy? It is plain to see that it is Jotham's allegory and not attested history.

"But how is a reader to discover which is which?" asked a curious student.

"How do you analyze ordinary literature?" I replied. "It is by context and a hundred and one other factors. That is why we organize a Bible class, to share the accumulation of ideas in interpretation. Augustine of Hippo declared that 'Scripture is what Scripture means.' "

Varieties of Inspiration

Many difficulties of interpretation are simply due to the fact that the ordinary reader has not been made aware that there are varieties of inspiration in the Scriptures. Six, at least, can be enumerated.

Let us take three terms, *revelation, inspiration*, and *illumination*. *Revelation*, in this instance, is defined as the words of God, directly disclosed; *inspiration*, in this case, as a concept relayed through the mind or soul of man; and *illumination*, in this relation, a spiritual or intellectual enlightenment based upon reflection or experience.

There are striking instances of revelation without inspiration, as in the giving of the Ten Commandments, or where the word of the Lord came to Ezekiel, saying: "Son of man, set your face toward the mountains of Israel and prophesy against them."[9]

With John, on the island of Patmos, the communication was received differently, when he was "in the Spirit on the Lord's day." This appeared to be revelation with inspiration, having elements of both.[10]

Quite a different set of circumstances prevailed[11] when Dr. Luke compiled his account of the life of Jesus Christ. It is impossible not to conclude that the Evangelist worked as a careful scholar, collecting material, interviewing eyewitnesses, collating information, and writing systematically—procedures to be considered inspiration without revelation.

Likewise in the First Letter to the Corinthians one finds illumination without inspiration. Referring to the inadvisability of contracting marriage during a vicious persecution of the Christians, the Apostle clearly states that he has no commandment from the Lord, but gives his opinion as one who is trustworthy. He stresses his lack of commandment also regarding advice to married couples.[12]

In the same Letter, illumination with inspiration occurs. The Apostle claimed that the Holy Spirit had taught him the things that he was teaching his converts,[13] combining both elements, illumination, and inspiration.

It is startling to some Christians to find in Scripture an example of inspiration without illumination. Yet that is precisely what is implied in the First Epistle of Peter, where prophets of old, who prophesied concerning Christ, did not know particularly to whom they were referring, their words being inspired but their minds unenlightened.[14]

If, instead of making Scripture fit one's own theories of inspiration, one makes such theories of inspiration fit the variety of Scripture, a great benefit is gained.

Interpretation of Scripture

More than one student has said to me:

"Why is it that I find so much of Scripture uninteresting?"

A lady of Norwegian birth attended the meetings of an Irish-born evangelist in the South African city of Durban, and, enjoying the ministry, notified her daughter a hundred miles away that she was staying on, which delay imposed additional duties on her daughter in the home. When she returned, the lady brought her daughter a set of the books published by the evangelist, but they lay unread for quite a while. She thought they must be uninteresting.

Later, the young lady, a telephone operator, spent a short vacation in Johannesburg and attended all the meetings of the same evangelist. To make a long story short, the young evangelist found himself greatly attracted, and finally proposed marriage to the girl who, upon her quick return to home and parents, asked immediately:

"Where are those books you brought me?"

With her closer acquaintance with the author, she found his published writings much more interesting.

The end of the story was, in classic language, "they lived happily ever after." This story I can certify personally!

Others have inquired why it is that Christians disagree so much in the interpretation of Scripture.

While serving with the Bethel Band in China during the awakening of 1927–39, I asked my colleague Andrew Gih if the Chinese Christians found themselves frustrated by the multiplicity of Western denominations.

"Yes, indeed," he replied. "In North China, there are Southern Baptists, and in South China there are Northern Baptists. In my native province, there were Baptists who baptized by immersion, Methodists who baptized by sprinkling, and Quakers who did not baptize at all."

"What distinction did the Chinese Christians make?"

"We call them," he explained, "the big-wash, and the little-wash, and the no-wash-at-all Christians."

It is true that Christians often differ in their interpretation of the Scriptures, and appeal in varying degree to the sacred words to support their case; but the area of their difference is very much smaller than supposed, full agreement on the greater issues being taken for granted.

The Bible Says . . .

During a moving of the Spirit among a thousand students at a conference at Forest Home, high in the San Bernardino Mountains of California in 1949, a platform colleague came to me long after midnight to discuss the question of commitment. Unknown to me, his mind was torn about the matter of the integrity and authority of Scripture. He went out into the woods to pray, and there he said:[15]

"Oh, God, I cannot prove certain things. I cannot answer some of the questions people are raising, but I accept this Book by faith as the Word of God."

That was a climactic moment in the life of the evangelist, William Franklin Graham. Within a month, he was making headlines nationally and internationally as a preacher of the Word of God. His understanding of it increased as he fully obeyed the light already received.

It is not enough, however, to claim the Scriptures as the authority for the believer. The Holy Spirit was promised to guide believers into all truth, the Spirit who also moved the men of old to write the words recorded; hence He can illuminate the mind and warm the heart of the obedient Christian in his search for guidance. His illumination is dimmed only by our dullness of perception.

CHAPTER THIRTEEN

Science and Scripture

It has already been shown that there is no conflict between the concept of God and the conclusions of science. But this declaration of "no case" does not automatically apply to the relation of science and Scripture, which must be examined.

However, the majority of objections to the scientific validity of Scripture may be resolved by consideration of science and Scripture as distinct from scientific theories and biblical interpretations. The following outline may help to simplify this resolution:[1]

God's

WORK	WORD
Science	Scripture
FACTS	TEXTS
Theories	Interpretations

God's work is discovered by us through science; God's word is revealed to us through Scripture; science is based upon facts so discovered; Scripture is composed of texts so revealed; scientists present scientific theories to explain the facts; Bible teachers offer interpretations to explain the texts. In the majority of cases, a conflict between science and Scripture may be resolved by reexamining the scientific theories and comparing with the facts, or by reexamining the biblical interpretations and comparing with the texts. It goes without saying that scientific theories without number have been jettisoned and forgotten; and that biblical interpretations likewise have been scrapped.

For example, it was once taught authoritatively that the planet Earth was surrounded by a medium carrying radio waves named ether; it was once taught authoritatively that the planet Earth was surrounded by a solid vault, designated the firmament. Scientists found that the theoretical ether was nonexistent, and Bible students realized that the expression translated "firmament" was better translated "atmosphere" or "space" —*raqia* meaning "stretched out" and not solid.

Students of Scripture often ask the popular question: "Is the first chapter of Genesis to be regarded as myth or as history?" The answer is neither, if by myth is meant a legend without reality, and if by history is meant the account of past events based upon reliable human testimony. The only definition of myth that seems to apply to the story of Creation in Genesis is "a story that attempts to explain a basic truth" but, because of the popular idea of myth being contrary to reality, the description "pictorial representation" is better used. And obviously, there was no human witness making notes when the Almighty declared: "Let there be light!" Thus the truth presented in the story of Creation is therefore considered revealed truth.

Legends of Creation?

Unbelieving teachers are often heard comparing the first chapter of Genesis with the legends of creation found in other religions.

It is most fashionable to derive the Genesis account from the Babylonian legends.[2] The Babylonian epic of creation taught that, in the beginning, there were two Gods only, Apsu and Tiamat, the latter a female dragon. Both lived in chaos, and from their cohabitation sprang all the gods of heaven and earth. These lesser gods rebelled against chaotic disorder, and sought to create an orderly universe. The male god of chaos, Apsu, was defeated by the god Ea, who became the deity of water. But Tiamat, the female god of chaos, chased both Ea, the water god, and Anu, the god of heaven. The gods then elevated to highest rank the son of Ea, Marduk, who battled with Tiamat and her eleven monsters, her armies and her husband. He defeated the hosts of Tiamat, chained the monsters to the stars, and divided the body of Tiamat into the vault of heaven and the habitation of earth, making man from the blood of her husband. Any comparison between Germanic or Babylonian legends and the magnificent language of Genesis is farfetched indeed.

Nowhere is this seen better than in a careful examination of the Creation story in the first chapter of Genesis and the three verses following. Far from being a rehashing of ancient myths, it can be demonstrated that the story of the Creation is a pictorial representation demonstrating a most remarkable harmony with the conclusions of modern science.

While engaged in postgraduate study in the earth sciences at Northwestern University, I asked Prof. Harold B. Ward whether he as a scientist found the Genesis account of the Creation repugnant to modern conclusions. Quite the contrary, he replied, adding that he was amazed by the degree of scientific accuracy in the poetic presentation.

Sequence in Creation

What does the first chapter of Genesis teach? How could it be summarized in modern English?

The story of Creation affirms that God created first the heaven and the earth; then caused light to radiate; then made an atmosphere between the clouds and the seas; then separated the land masses from the ocean; next delegated to the earth the power to produce vegetation, made celestial clocks to function for seasons; caused the oceans to produce animal life, developed birds to populate the troposphere, caused the earth to bring forth its animals, and gave man dominion over plants and animals.[3]

It is worthy of note that the Hebrew word *bara* ("create") is used only three times in the Genesis account, in creation of the material universe, in creation of animal life, and in creation of spiritual man. These three instances coincide with three scientific mysteries, unanswered to date—the origin of the material universe, the appearance of life, and the appearance of homo sapiens or spiritual man.[4]

What about the other developments? In the Genesis story, the verbs of indirect action appear: *make, form, let there be, let the earth bring forth, let the waters bring forth*, all of them mediate rather than immediate.

A conservative churchman adhering to some modification of the Ussher view of Creation, told me in discussion:

"When God created the first tree, He must have made it with a certain number of rings—let us say a hundred. Then it looked a hundred years old, when in fact it was only an afternoon old!"

I pointed out to him that the Scripture did not say

that God had created a tree. Instead it clearly indicated that God had commanded the earth to bring forth grass, bushes and fruit trees, a poetic way of saying vegetation primitive, intermediate, and highly developed. To me, it seemed clear that God had delegated the power to the earth, and that the vegetating of the earth was a process rather than an act.

The Days of Decree

Inevitably, the problem of the "days" of Genesis arises. Some insist that these days represent literal, twenty-four-hour days, contradicting the conclusions of earth scientists as well as opinion in the early Church, as seen in Augustine of Hippo's declaration that "the length of these days is not to be determined by the length of our week days; there is a series in both cases and that is all." Augustine's cosmology is not binding on any Christian today, but his remark shows clearly that the nonliteral interpretation of the "days" was current in the early Church.

Attempts have been made to equate the days of Genesis with the great geological ages. The difficulty lies in trying to make them fit periods which began and ended with times that are calculable. The order set forth in Genesis seems to be a logical one, rather than a chronological account of a scientific nature.

Others have presented the Genesis time divisions as "days of dictation"[5] by the scribe of Genesis; or as "days of revelation"; or the like. I much prefer *days of decree*, but that is a term that calls for explanation.

There was a day of guaranteed personal liberty dawning on the English-speaking world on 15 June 1215, when the Magna Carta was signed; that day has not yet concluded! On the Fourth of July 1776, a new day dawned in North America, one of independence; that day has not concluded. On the First of January 1863, a new day dawned in the United States of America, with the proclamation of the emancipation of the slaves by President Lincoln; that day has not concluded. These days began with a decree, and have not yet ended.[6]

Objections have been raised that the repeated expression "the evening and the morning were the first day . . . second day . . ." and so on, limits the day to twenty-four hours. It is generally recognized that where this expression occurs in the Book of Daniel it has a figurative meaning; in Genesis it is cryptic. Some scholars have thought of the repetition as liturgical, a response of the congregation to the reading of the minister. In Hebrew thought, the evening marked the beginning of the day, the morning the end. The minimum of meaning is surely that there was a beginning of action and an end of accomplishment. When the purpose of God was fulfilled, the action ended, but its results continued fully effective. The light yet shone, the atmosphere functioned still, the land masses remained above the oceans, and the earth-produced vegetation still propagated itself.

Those who advocate equating the "days" with geological ages and those who consider them "days of decree" alike encounter an objection "that the sun and moon were created on the fourth day." The literal interpretation does not bother those who attribute their creation to a period between the seventy-second and ninety-sixth hour of the age of the earth; a problem is presented for those who think otherwise. How can the first-day commandment "Let there be light!" be made to agree with the fourth-day creation of the sun and moon? Textual interpretation provides an alternative.[7]

The six short verses that describe the accomplishments of the fourth day nowhere state that God created the sun and moon subsequent to the making of an atmosphere or the separation of the land masses or the beginning of vegetation. The verb *create* is not used. The sun and moon were made to shine. The sense of the passage is that the sun and moon were made to function as the measurers of days and weeks and months and seasons and years; and the conditions that presently prevail on the planet Venus help to explain this idea that there was a time when the light of sun and moon was not functional, but became so when the cloud cover was dissipated in the course of time.

Let us therefore examine the first full statement of the story of Creation, found in the first two verses of the first chapter of Genesis, given as a single, connected statement in the original:

"In the beginning, God created the heaven and the earth. And the earth was without form and void; and darkness was upon the face of the deep. And the Spirit of God moved upon the face of the waters."

Modern Cosmogony

The 1971 translation of the Bible, paraphrased by fellow alumnus Kenneth N. Taylor, has offered as an alternative to "the face of the waters"[8] "the dark vapors" or "the cloud of darkness." It could be read thus: "When God began creating the heaven and the earth, the earth was at first a shapeless mass, with the Spirit of God brooding over the dark cloud."

It is obvious that the translators appointed by James

I in 1604 adopted the cosmogony of the sixteenth century, just as most modern translators reflect the cosmogony of the twentieth century. No translation of ancient Babylonian or other legends could effect a harmony with the scientific conclusions of today, nor could the myths of the Aztecs or Teutons, the Japanese, or Hindus.

The article on cosmogony in the leading encyclopedia provides an up-to-date review of scientific conclusions on the subject.[9] Although the theories of a steady-state cosmos and of a fluctuating state are considered, it is still the real consensus of scientific opinion that the observable universe had a beginning, billions of years ago. This is arrived at by half a dozen lines of reasoning, and does not conflict at all with the simple scriptural statement, "In the beginning, God created—" The alternative cosmologies produce not one item of evidence in support.

What are the theories of leading scientists, briefly stated? Enrico Fermi, who achieved the first atomic chain reaction, taught that the end of the thermonuclear explosion which started the universe resulted in gas clouds which were 99 percent hydrogen and helium, the remaining 1 percent containing heavier elements, including deuterium. It was his view that these elements were created in the first thirty minutes of the existence of the universe, a staggering observation.

I was hitchhiking once across Micronesia, and stopped a while at an Air Force base as a guest of veteran combat. For some reason or other, the occupants of the officers' quarters arose before the dawn had broken. The noise they made prevented me from sleeping further, so I too arose and followed them down to the landing. No one seemed at all willing to acquaint me with the reasons for watching for the dawn, so I waited patiently. Sure enough, there was a gasp as a lightening glow spread across the sky. But I realized it was the western sky. The early light of dawn died down again, and only then did I discover that a thermonuclear bomb had been exploded farther west.[10]

Atomic explosions of today create their dangerous and deadly elements, such as strontium-90, in a microsecond, a millionth of a second. Thus I could understand Enrico Fermi's claim, though thirty minutes make a startling fraction of the age of the universe.

The primal superexplosion hurled clouds of lighter gas outwards in progressive expansion; thus there was thin gas throughout the universe, clouds in gravitational instability, with no aggregation of heavier matter for a quarter of a billion years. These expanding gas clouds formed the cold, proto galaxies, the galaxies of stars being yet unformed. Many of the best astronomers have held that the stars were formed in these gas clouds by condensation caused by gravity and by radiation, stellar radiation bringing new stars into being.[11]

Extraterrestrial Life?

At a time when the reading public suffers from a surfeit of speculation about extraterrestrial life, civilizations on other planets outside the solar system, flying saucers and the like, it is astounding to realize that to date astronomers have discovered not a single other solar system than our own. Speculation on other inhabited planets is not based upon the evidence of sight or sound, photography or radio.

For many years, it was customary for student questioners to cite the case of Barnard's star and its dark companion. True, it had not been proved that the dark companion was a planet; it could have been a dead star circling a sun. That only one such example of anything resembling a planetary body outside our solar system had been discovered did not discourage the wild speculations of science writers.[12]

Then came the revelation that the dark companion of Barnard's star had never actually been seen in a telescope or located by its radio waves by any means whatsoever. In fact, it was decided that the dark companion did not exist, and that the aberration of rotation in Barnard's star could be accounted for without inventing another celestial body.[13]

So far, then, it is necessary to account for the origin of only one solar system. The others exist only in imagination and their inhabitants are creatures of science fiction. But the origin of the one and only solar system known to man is still a subject to interest astronomers, philosophers, and, of course, theologians.

The Solar System

The French scientist, Pierre-Simon Laplace, suggested that the solar system was formed from a solar nebula that was condensing by rotation.[14] After it was shown that a disk of matter of uniform density would break up into rings resembling those of Saturn rather than individual planets, the hypothesis presented by Immanuel Kant suffered an eclipse that lasted long. Until 1944, a collision theory popularized by Sir James Jeans attracted much attention and won considerable support, it being suggested that a wandering star had nearly collided with the Sun and torn off parts which settled into steady orbits as the familiar planets. It was then proposed and demonstrated that rejection of Kant's hypothesis had been based on misinterpretation, for the solar nebula could not have been of uniform density, the solar system having been demonstrated as otherwise. Von Weizsäcker postulated a solar nebula condensing into 99 percent hydrogen and helium, and only 1 percent terrestrial elements.

Since 1944, there has been fairly general agreement about the origin of the solar system. The most modern theory was refined by Gerhard Kuiper of the University of Arizona, famed for his work in the moon project initiated by President Kennedy and successfully completed.[15]

"The important point of Kuiper's theory," declared Prof. George Gamow, noted physicist, "is that the formation of the protoplanets took place in darkness before the sun was sufficiently condensed to emit light." Thus modern science arrived at a conclusion which was anticipated by Holy Writ; in fact, the only qualifying statement made about the earth in its earliest ages, that it was without form and void and enveloped in darkness, is thus confirmed.

The Song of Creation

It is the fashion nowadays for scientific experts to smile indulgently when mention is made of a biblical cosmogony; and for theologians also to protest attempts to reconcile the story told in Genesis with up-to-date astronomy. Could it be that scientists know little of interpretation of the Word and theologians even less of up-to-date astronomy?

The fact remains that Genesis, unlike the legends of the ancient past, presents a revelation of the power of God in primal creation, a prose poem of beauty and of majesty to explain the first great Cause. Genesis is not a scientific text, but rather a song of creation.[16]

CHAPTER FOURTEEN

The Self-Revelation of God

It comes as a shock to many students to discover how little humanity knows about God by media other than the Scriptures. Science tells us practically nothing about God; in philosophy, one man's speculation seems to be as good as another's. The gods of pantheism and polytheism seem to be projections of man's passion at its best and its worst.

But, in the realm of science, our knowledge of God in nature would lead us to expect a revelation of truth which would not contradict what we have learned from nature. As nature teaches its lessons in graded steps, one may expect in revelation a continuous development of the truth.

One of the first of the difficulties that comes to mind is the question, how is anyone to distinguish a human philosophy from a divine revelation, to refuse a notion of someone's mind and accept a revelation from the Deity?

A message of God's truth should be recognizable by the marks of its divine authorship. Divinely inspired writings should record the sins and failures of its human heroes, in contrast to the eulogies that human vanity promotes. Divinely inspired writers should be attested by marks of the divine communication—by the prophetic and the miraculous.

All this is uniquely true of Holy Scripture. And it is likewise significant that the best method of preserving a divine revelation is by means of written record rather than oral communication alone. The written record was passed on by copyists noted for their meticulous care attributable to their recognition of the divine revelation.

The sixty-six books of the Holy Bible, though written by many authors over many centuries, constitute a great work in the science of humanity, but appear to all students of the message to be the work of one Mind, with a unity of spirit, subject, and object throughout. True, the message has been mediated through men in very varied circumstances, from royalty to fisherman. But it is possessed of a unity, without doubt. It is not inappropriate to state: "The Bible says . . ." in the latter half of the twentieth century.

God in the Absolute

What does this divine library teach about God? First of all, His absolute attributes— that God is spirit, infinite, and perfect.[1] The texts are familiar: "God is spirit"; "the heaven of heavens cannot contain Thee!"; and "Your heavenly Father is perfect." It is obvious that science could not ascertain these facts for us.

Scripture teaches that God's spirituality is expressed in life, energy, and personality, and again the phrases are familiar: "the living God"; "God is light"; and God describes Himself as the "I am."[2]

Scripture teaches that God's infinity is expressed in His self-existence, changelessness, and unity.[3] The words are plain: "I am that I am"—that is, self-existing; "I the Lord change not"—that is, changeless; and "the Lord our God is one Lord!"—that is, unified.

Scripture teaches that God's perfection is expressed in truth, love, and holiness.[4] The statements are simple: God is "the only true . . ."; "God is love!"; "Holy, holy, holy is the Lord of hosts."

Thus one finds a triad of triads for the absolute attributes of God: God is spirit—life, energy, and personality; God is infinite—self-existing, changeless, and one; and God is perfect—in truth, love, and holiness. These attributes are absolute in God Himself without reference to any other.

God in the Relative

The relative attributes of God are stated in Scripture in relation to the material universe, to all living creatures, and to moral beings, again a triad of triads.

Scripture states quite plainly, by divine self-revelation, that God is immense—greater than the universe, for "the heaven of heavens" cannot contain Him; God is eternal—"from everlasting . . . Thou art God!"; God is incorporeal,—not limited to a body, "the invisible God."[5] Scripture states that, in relation to life, God is omnipotent, omniscient, and omnipresent—"God Almighty" . . . "all things open to His eyes" . . . does He not "fill heaven and earth"?[6] And in relation to moral beings, God is truthful and faithful, God is merciful and good, God is just and righteous.[7] And the texts cited are not odd verses; the truths explicitly stated are fundamental throughout the sixty-six books.

Scientifically Disqualified?

Does the self-revelation of God disqualify itself in the light of science, of soundly based scientific conclusions? The question must be asked in relation to cosmology, to teleology, and to anthropology.

Is there any fact or scientific conclusion in the realm of cosmology which would rule out the concept of a Creator Who is pure spirit—invisible, indivisible, and indestructible; Who is infinite—boundless, not even bounded by the universe; Who is perfect—not merely quantitatively complete, but qualitatively excellent? The answer obviously is no! Does the self-revelation of God as spirit, infinite and perfect, provide any answer to the unanswered question of cosmology, the origin of the universe? To quote a modern philosopher, at first sight it offers us what is "the most plausible account of some of the most pervasive, exciting and extraordinary aspects of our existence and our environment; and it provides us with answers to a large number of questions . . . where did the universe come from?"[8] And there is nothing in cosmology to disqualify the existence of a Being greater than the universe, a proposition based upon the immensity of God, one of His relative attributes.

Is there any fact or scientific conclusion in the realm of teleology which would rule out the concept of a Designer Who is spirit, infinite, and perfect? Again the answer is no! And does this self-revelation provide any answer to the unanswered question of teleology, design in nature? To quote the same philosopher, "Could there have been a Designer . . . a Being which gave form to all the Universe and which derived its own form from nothing outside itself . . . ?" "Indeed there could."[9] But he went on to say that this proposition was disqualified because it did not answer the question of the origin of the Designer! That God is omnipotent, omniscient, and omnipresent makes more sense than suggesting that "out of a purposeless universe has come purpose," which does not make sense.

Is there any fact or scientific conclusion in the realm of anthropology which would rule out the concept of a Lawgiver Who is spirit, infinite and perfect? Again the answer is no! And does this self-revelation provide any answer to the unanswered question of anthropology, the origin of morality? God, self-revealed as true, good, and just, provides the most satisfying answer to the problem.

Objective Assent

Some who have noted that the skeptics have produced no disqualification at all of the revelation of God have gone on from there to take, not a leap in the dark, but a step to a position clearly seen, a step of faith, and have experienced the reality of God. Far more of us have already enjoyed a convincing experience of the reality of God but have met with a challenge to our faith and have willingly walked with the skeptics over the rocky ground of their objections, our faith having been strengthened thereby.

It cannot be said too strongly, however, that our faith in God is no mere assent to a set of propositions. Rather, our knowledge of God comes to us through a divine self-revelation; it is congenial to reason, but it is verified by personal experience. And with this personal experience comes the illumination of the Holy Spirit; for the ordinary man does not understand spiritual things, they sound foolish to him, for spiritual things are spiritually discerned.

Once a man has been born again, once his mind has been enlightened, the fact of God fits in with all his experience of life. His faith sheds light upon his every observation of nature. Again and again, one finds a believing physician marveling at the wonders of the human body, or a believing chemist astounded by the wonders of chemistry; whereas the unbelieving expert seems to study his field with a very strange indifference towards the explanation of the ultimate; and the expert who has rejected God seems to seek for the farthest-fetched alternatives with a zeal that is far from being scientifically objective.

Sad to say, many skeptics possess a vested interest in unbelief,[10] for faith would radically change their life-style. Hence, some who profess to be wise become fools, and the innocents inherit the kingdom instead.

CHAPTER FIFTEEN

The Unsurpassed Revelation of God

Time and again, students have told me: "My problem is not believing in some kind of God. It is believing in the deity of Christ." That kind of statement is very revealing, for it is not enough to believe in some kind of God—such as an impersonal "ground of all being," but in the God and Father of our Lord Jesus Christ.

Occasionally, some ill-informed person has stated in public debate that "historians generally speaking have discarded the historicity of Jesus."[1] This is no great handicap in debate, for the correction of such a notion is certain to show that the speaker has not done his homework. No serious scholar for a long time has postulated the nonhistoricity of Jesus, and non-Christian historians readily agree that Jesus is as historic as Julius Cæsar or any other man of his times.

It is true that there is little in contemporary secular writings about Christ, but it is enough to supplement the score of Christian sources for His life. Flavius Josephus, Cornelius Tacitus, Suetonius Tranquillus, Plinius Secundus, and others made supporting statements.[2] But the wealth of information naturally is found in the New Testament, whose authenticity has been established. Careless debaters who toy with a "Christ-myth" should note that the encyclopedias devote twenty-thousand words to Jesus Christ.[3]

The Unique Personality

Among non-Christians, Jean-Jacques Rousseau declared "if the life and death of Socrates are those of a philosopher, the life and death of Jesus Christ are those of a God."[4] He was, as Sholem Asch remarked, "the outstanding personality of all time."[5] Napoleon Bonaparte, reflecting, said of Jesus: "Between him and every other person . . . there is no possible comparison; . . . at this hour, millions of men would die for him." H. G. Wells, popular scientist and historian, stated that "Jesus stands first" in making a permanent impression on history. He was the most influential man on earth.

His Claims to Deity

More than once, objectors have told me that the claim to deity was not made by Jesus, but was foisted on His simple followers by later systematic theologians, such as Paul the Apostle. One such dismissed the statement made by Jesus, "I and the Father are one," by saying that any child of God could say that; but I reminded my Harvard friend that he could not claim, "He who has seen me has seen the Father." Likewise, His fellow countrymen did not misunderstand Him when He declared that "I and my Father are one," for they immediately took up stones to stone Him, and told Him bluntly that it was for blasphemy, "because you, being a man, make yourself God." The Greek text makes clear that Jesus claimed to be one in essence or nature with God.[6]

The record of the trial of Jesus before the high priest is sure. The high priest asked Him bluntly: "Are you the Christ, the Son of the Blessed?" And Jesus answered very plainly: "I am; and you will see the Son of Man sitting at the right hand of power and coming in the clouds of heaven," so significant a declaration that the High Priest declared no need of further witnesses, for all had heard the blasphemy, and they judged Him guilty of death. It seems conclusive that Jesus and His judges alike sought an opportunity of making public, once and for all, His claims to deity.[7]

When his countrymen sarcastically reminded Him that He was not fifty years old, hence how could He have seen Abraham, Jesus replied gratuitously, "Before Abraham was, I am."[8] Again, they threatened to stone Him, for such a declaration was a claim to preexistence and more, a claim to timelessness.

Unlike the prophets, whose greatest mark of authority lay in the words, "Thus saith the Lord," the Lord Jesus prefaced His teaching with the words, "Verily, verily, I say unto you." He announced unabashedly,[9] "Heaven and earth will pass away, but My words will not pass away." He never hesitated, modified, withdrew, or apologized for His words.

Recognized as Deity

Jesus Christ spoke unequivocally as Deity, and this fact was recognized by friend and foe alike, according to record. John, the Evangelist, was a devout young Jew who knew well the Hebrew antipathy towards claimants of deity. At some stage or other of his life, he must have come to the conclusion that this young prophet of Nazareth, Jesus, was more than an ordinary man.

The introduction to the Gospel of John begins with

the words:[10] "In the beginning was the Word, and the Word was with God, and the Word was God." The Word (Logos) is unanimously referred to Christ. The introductory statement is a declaration of deity, the first phrase speaking of His eternity, the second of His personality, and the third of His deity. The third phrase has been troublesome to the Jehovah's Witnesses, who claim that the lack of a definite article before the Greek word *theos* denotes a lesser god. The Greek experts uniformly deny this, and translate the phrase "and the Word was deity."[11]

Thomas, the doubting apostle, suddenly recognized the risen Christ, and exclaimed, "My Lord and my God!"—the Greek expression including the definite article this time. The writer to the Hebrews applies the title of God to the Son in no cryptic way.[12]

The Apostle Paul had received the strictest training in Jewish theology, besides being a scholar in Greek and Latin. Yet he did not hesitate to refer to the appearing of "our great God and Savior Jesus Christ."[13] There are other clear references to the deity of Christ in Paul's epistles.

Attributes of Deity

The writers of the New Testament adapt the words of the prophet Isaiah about "the way of the Lord" and "the glory of the Lord" to Christ, and angels told to worship Him in the Psalms are cited in Hebrews in reference to Christ.[14]

It has been noted that life and changelessness are among the absolute attributes of God.[15] New Testament writers have ascribed these to Jesus Christ—"in

Him was life," and "the power of an endless life"; and "Jesus Christ, the same yesterday, today and forever."[16]

The relative attributes of God—truth, love, and holiness—are likewise ascribed to Christ.[17] So are omnipotence, omniscience, and omnipresence.[18] To Him is ascribed the work of creation, and the sustaining of creation.[19] Honor and worship and glory are offered Him.[20]

It is surely noteworthy that the New Testament writers applied the titles of the Almighty as given in the Psalms and Prophets to Jesus Christ—Creator, Savior, Judge, Light, Shepherd, Redeemer, Bridegroom, and the like—as well as adapting references to raising the dead, forgiving sinners, addressed in prayer, and confessed as Lord.

Birth, Life, Death, Resurrection

Eli Stanley Jones once startled his vast audience at the Maramon Convention in India by declaiming:

"I do not believe in the deity of Christ . . ."

He waited for his interpreter, and the audience waited.

". . . because of the virgin birth."

Still there was suspense.

"Rather," explained the Methodist, "I believe in the virgin birth because I believe in the deity of Christ. Accepting the doctrine of the deity of Christ, I do not find it difficult to believe that he had an unusual entrance into this life and an unusual exit from it."

The story of the miraculous birth of Jesus is given by the Evangelists Matthew and Luke in convincing detail. The historical reference in these accounts to the Roman

Census is attested.[21] Jesus Himself bore witness to the circumstances of His birth in His repeated use of the words, "the only begotten Son." The early church—apart from minor sects—wholeheartedly accepted the doctrine.

The life of Christ is without peer. He challenged his opponents to point a finger at a single sin. Most followers of heroes are ready to admit the human frailties of their leader. The disciples found no fault to concede. Nor did his enemies other than that of the claim to deity.

Despite the strange Islamic denial of His crucifixion, it is the verdict of history that Jesus Christ was crucified—even the Roman records support this.[22] The accounts of the crucifixion are fourfold, the so-called discrepancies inconsequent but more convincing than would be identical accounts.

It is not too much to claim that, all the evidence considered, there is no historic incident better supported than the resurrection of Christ. The various stories proposed to deny the resurrection are either fatuous or contradictory. Added to the testimony of the apostles and of more than four hundred witnesses is the experience of generations of believers—who share convincing experience that He is alive.

About the Author

Irish-born of an American father and British mother, J. Edwin Orr received his elementary education in Ireland and proceeded to the College of Technology in Belfast, but was forced to abandon his studies in order to support his widowed mother and family. He spent six years in business.

In 1933, at the bottom of the Depression, he left home on a bicycle and visited every part of England, Scotland, Wales, and Ireland, having no means of support other than providential guidance. He then visited the northern countries of Europe en route to the USSR and returned via the Baltic, Germany, and the Low Countries. Next he visited Southern Europe and Palestine.

In 1935, Edwin Orr traversed Canada from Newfoundland to British Columbia, addressing crowds in Toronto's Massey Hall and elsewhere. He visited each of the United States of America, addressing eager audiences in all the big cities, including ten thousand in Chicago's Coliseum. From the West Indies, he journeyed to New Zealand and Australia, thence to South Africa, still working as a layman.

In 1937, Orr married Ivy Carol Carlson, of Norwegian parentage, in South Africa. In 1938, he engaged in work in the war zones of China with the Bethel Bands. In 1939, he became associate minister of the Peoples Church in Toronto. In 1940, he returned to higher education, at Northwestern University and half a dozen theological graduate schools in Illinois, completing his doctorate.

In 1942, Orr was commissioned in the air force, and served four years in uniform, chiefly in the U.S. Thirteenth Air Force in the Southwest Pacific, from Guadalcanal to Tokyo. He hitchhiked 24,000 miles to study at Oxford—crossing the length of Asia and Africa en route. In 1948, he was graduated with the D.Phil. at Oxford University.

In 1949, Orr was engaged chiefly in student ministry in the United States and Canada, witnessing stirring times of spiritual awakening. In 1952, he campaigned throughout the states of Brazil in a nationwide movement of awakening; he also visited all the countries of the Americas. In 1953, he ministered throughout Africa, visiting every country. In 1954, he began a series of visits to India, and addressed more than a million people there. He visited all the countries of Asia. To date, he has visited 150 of the world's 160 countries and two-thirds of all its major cities.

For the past ten years, Orr has served on the faculty of the School of World Mission at Fuller Theological Seminary, chiefly assisting missionaries and nationals from all over the world in postgraduate studies. He has also taught a course in apologetics in the School of Theology. Besides this work, he spends part of each year in universities and colleges, often sponsored by the Staley Foundation, and directs a consortium of scholars each summer at Oxford in the Oxford Reading and Research projects in evangelical awakenings, sponsored by the Archbishop of Canterbury and other denominational leaders.

Besides high academic awards from universities

overseas, Orr holds the doctor of education degree of the University of California at Los Angeles. He is the author of thirty books, some popular, others now used as standard texts in historical research. The presidents and principals of colleges report that his lectures are still noted for their appeal to student audiences.

Notes

Chapter 1. Science and the Fallacies

1. The names of people are fictitious, place names switched around.
2. Paul B. Weisz, *Elements of Biology*, p. 432.
3. *See also* A. H. Compton, *The Freedom of Man*, pp. 75ff.

Chapter 2. The Anatomy of Unbelief

1. Cf. Bertrand Russell, *Why I Am Not a Christian*.
2. T. H. Huxley, "Agnosticism," in *Science and the Christian Tradition*, New York, 1894.

Chapter 3. A Christian Case

1. H. P. Owen, *The Christian Knowledge of God*, pp. 135ff.
2. *See* Nathaniel Micklem, *A Religion for Agnostics*, p. 53: "All men are aware of God, but many do not realize that it is of God that they are aware."
3. John 14:9.
4. Tiberius, Pilate, Herod, Philip, Lysanius, Caiaphas, and Annas.
5. Interviewed by Dr. Carl F. H. Henry.
6. 1 Corinthians 15:6.
7. I Peter 3:15 (Berkeley).

Chapter 4. The Cosmological Argument

1. Benjamin Jowett, *Dialogues of Plato*, vol. 4, pp. 463ff.
2. Richard Hope, *Metaphysics*, p. 51.
3. Cf. F. C. Copleston, *Aquinas*, pp. 117ff.
4. See S. M. Thompson, *A Modern Philosophy of Religion*.
5. David Hume, *Dialogues Concerning Natural Religion*, part 9.

6. See B. R. Reichenbach, *The Cosmological Argument*, p. 97; "An infinite series of contingent beings is incapable of providing a sufficient reason for the existence of any being" (p. 11).

7. Cf. BBC broadcast debate, Russell & Copleston, Oxford, 1948, and F. C. Copleston, *Aquinas*, p. 127.

8. R. E. D. Clark, *The Universe: Plan or Accident?*, noted that all the universe is running down, and no rewinding is probable.

9. Richard Feynman, *Lectures on Physics*, California Institute of Technology, section 46-5.

10. Cf. H. F. Blum, *Time's Arrow and Evolution*, p. 16.

11. *New Encyclopaedia Britannica*, 1974, vol. 9, p. 540: "Observations since the 1950s have produced much evidence in contradiction" to the Steady-State hypothesis.

12. BBC broadcast debate, Russell & Copleston, Oxford, 1948.

13. Cf. John Hick, *Classical and Contemporary Readings in the Philosophy of Religion*, p. 468.

Chapter 5. The Teleological Argument

1. W. G. Pollard, *Chance and Providence*, pp. 92ff: "Chance cannot be a cause."

2. The Oxford professor is fictitious.

3. Prof. J. Fulford Jarvis, University of Cape Town, "The Universe—Chance or Design," Lecture, S.C.M., 1967.

4. Pierre Lecomte du Noüy, *Human Destiny*, pp. 26ff.

5. W. G. Pollard, *Chance and Providence*, pp. 79–80.

6. Michael Scriven, *Primary Philosophy*, p. 126.

7. Prof. J. Fulford Jarvis, "The Universe—Chance or Design."

8. William Paley, *Natural Theology*, chapters 1 and 2.

9. David Hume, *Dialogues Concerning Natural Religion*, part 5.

10. Hume conceded that Cleanthes was closer to the truth; and Kant neither disproved God nor disregarded the teleological arguments: D. A. Burrill, ed., *Cosmological Arguments*, p. 189.

11. Michael Scriven, *Primary Philosophy*, p. 127.

12. Miller and Orgel, *The Origins of Life*, pp. 83ff.

13. Michael Scriven, *Primary Philosophy*, p. 130.

14. Debate, Michael Scriven and J. Edwin Orr, Indiana University, 1965.

Chapter 6. The Anthropological Argument

1. In 1957, the writer toured Arnhem Land. Names are fictitious.
2. See H. P. Owen, *The Moral Argument for Christian Theism*, pp. 32ff.
3. Immanuel Kant, *Critique of Practical Reason*, from T. K. Abbott, *Kant's Theory of Ethics*, 1889.
4. "A moral ideal can exist nowhere and nohow but in a mind; an absolute moral ideal can exist only in a Mind from which all Reality is derived," Hastings Rashdall, *The Theory of Good and Evil*, vol. 2, p. 212.
5. See Principal Charles Duthie's summary of H. P. Owen, above, in *British Weekly*, London, 24 June 1965.

Chapter 7. Argument and Its Limits

1. S. N. Deane, *St. Anselm*, LaSalle, Illinois, 1948; cf. E. K. Fairweather, *A Scholastic Miscellany: Anselm to Ockham*, pp. 73–75.
2. See A. C. Pegis, *The Basic Writings of St. Thomas Aquinas*, New York, 1945.
3. René Descartes, *Principles of Philosophy*, Meditation 5; and Immanuel Kant, *Critique of Pure Reason*.
4. Blaise Pascal, *Pensées sur la religion*.
5. Michael Scriven, *Primary Philosophy*, p. 151. Dr. Scriven declared (whimsically) that he regarded "invincible doubt" as a valuable insurance policy for himself (Debate, 1965).
6. Principal Nathaniel Micklem, Oxford, private conversation.
7. See Blaise Pascal, *Pensées*, edition Brunschvicg, 4, p. 243.
8. Cf. John Baillie, *Our Knowledge of God*, pp. 119ff.
9. James 2:19–20.
10. Romans 1:20.

Chapter 8. Counterargument

1. See A. J. Ayer, *Language, Truth and Logic*, pp. 114ff.
2. *Time* Magazine, 5 June 1950, p. 82.

3. Symposium: "The Christian Answer in the World Dilemma," Oxford, Sir David Ross, C. S. Lewis, chairman Howard Guinness.
4. Ludwig Feuerbach, *The Essence of Christianity*, pp. 12ff, George Eliot translation.
5. Debate, Michael Scriven and J. Edwin Orr, Indiana University, 1965; cf. Michael Scriven, *Primary Philosophy*, p. 103.
6. Implication in John Hick, *The Existence of God*, p. 227.
7. H. J. Schonfield, *The Passover Plot*, New York, 1966; *see Jerusalem Post* Magazine, 23 April 1976, for an update.
8. John Wisdom, "Gods," in *Philosophy and Psycho-analysis*, Oxford, 1953; cf. Antony Flew and Alasdair MacIntyre, in *New Essays in Philosophical Theology*, p. 96.
9. Rheinallt Williams, *Faith, Facts, History, Science*, p. 32.
10. See M. E. Golay, *Analytical Chemistry*, June 1961.
11. Even Sir Julian Huxley conceded that—by his own calculations—the chances of evolution were represented by fifteen hundred pages of zeros, which my computer-expert friends thought very modest; *see* Julian Huxley, *Evolution in Action*, p. 46.

Chapter 9. The Problem of Evil

1. David Hume, *Dialogues Concerning Natural Religion*.
2. *See* Nelson Pike, ed., *God and Evil*, pp. 47 and 61.
3. "Shall Gravitation cease when you go by?" (Pope).
4. John Stuart Mill, *Three Essays on Religion*, p. 28.
5. E. J. Carnell, *Introduction to Christian Apologetics*, p. 302.
6. Cf. H. P. Black, "The Problem of Evil," *Christianity Today*, 23 April 1971, pp. 9ff.
7. Evangelical Christians were often Inquisition victims.

Chapter 10. Faith and Experience

1. Example given in debate, Michael Scriven and J. Edwin Orr, 1965.
2. My wife's doctor, Viola Fryman, a surgeon, showed X rays on TV of the growth—after prayer—of a femur by more than two inches.
3. See Rheinallt Williams, chapter 6.
4. Matthew 3:1; 4:17; Mark 6:12; Acts 2:38, 26:20.

Chapter 11. Attested Revelation

1. F. F. Bruce, *The New Testament Documents*, pp. 16ff.
2. F. F. Bruce, *The Books and the Parchments*, p. 183.
3. F. G. Kenyon, *The Bible and Modern Scholarship*, p. 20.
4. Philip Schaff, *Companion to the Greek New Testament*.
5. F. F. Bruce, *The Books and the Parchments*, pp. 179–80.

Chapter 12. Inspiration of Scripture

1. 2 Timothy 3:16.
2. Thomas Jefferson, *The Life and Morals of Jesus of Nazareth*, compiled 1816, printed 1904.
3. 1 Corinthians 1:14–16.
4. 2 Timothy 3:16.
5. Matthew 1:23 and Luke 1:27.
6. 1 Thessalonians 5:2–4 and 2 Thessalonians 2:1–2.
7. Psalm 23.
8. Judges 9:8–15.
9. Exodus 20:1–17; Ezekiel 6:1–2.
10. Revelation 1:10.
11. Luke 1:1–4.
12. 1 Corinthians 7:25–26, 5–6.
13. 1 Corinthians 2:13.
14. 1 Peter 1:10–12.
15. *Christianity Today*, 15 October 1956.

Chapter 13. Science and Scripture

1. Outline from Dr. Alton Everest, Moody Institute of Science.
2. *See* S. H. Langdon, *The Babylonian Epic of Creation*.
3. Genesis 1:1, 3, 6, 9, 11, 14, 20, 21, 24, 28.
4. Genesis 1:1, 21, 27.
5. *See* P. J. Wiseman, *Creation Revealed in Six Days*.
6. So far as one can ascertain, the term *days of decree* has been used previously by no one else.
7. Cf. F. A. Filby, *Creation Revealed*, p. 70.
8. K. N. Taylor, *The Living Bible*, Genesis 1:1 and footnote.
9. George Gamow, in *Encyclopaedia Britannica*, 1958, vol. 6: pp. 498ff.
10. Thermonuclear test, Eniwetok, 1 March 1954, seen from Kwajalein in the Marshall Islands.

11. *New Encyclopaedia Britannica, Micropaedia,* vol. 2, p. 10 (big-bang hypothesis).
12. *Astronomical Journal,* vol. 74, 1969, p. 241.
13. *Astronomical Journal,* vol. 78, 1973, p. 769.
14. Pierre-Simon Laplace (1796) postulated a cold, dark nebula (*New Encyclopaedia Britannica,* vol. 10, pp. 1031–1032), an idea developed by Immanuel Kant.
15. See G. P. Kuiper and B. M. Middlehurst, *The Solar System,* 4 vols., 1953–1963.
16. Cf. Psalm 104.

Chapter 14. The Self-Revelation of God

1. John 4:24; 1 Kings 8:27; Matthew 5:48.
2. Jeremiah 10:10; 1 John 1:5; Exodus 3:14.
3. Exodus 3:14; Malachi 3:6; Deuteronomy 6:4.
4. John 17:3; 1 John 4:8; Isaiah 6:3.
5. 1 Kings 8:27; Psalm 90:2; Colossians 1:15.
6. Genesis 17:1; Hebrews 4:13; Jeremiah 23:24.
7. Romans 4:3 and 1 Corinthians 1:9; Psalm 52:8 and Romans 2:4; Genesis 18:25 and Lamentations 1:18.
8. Debate, Michael Scriven & J. Edwin Orr, Indiana University, 1965.
9. Michael Scriven, *Primary Philosophy*, p. 130.
10. Ardent atheists, from Hume to Russell, have been careless in their sexual morals. Of course, sexual chastity is not the only ideal. It is noteworthy that atheists as a class are seldom philanthropic.

Chapter 15. The Unsurpassed Revelation of God

1. Debate, Leslie Armour, editor of *Ubyssey,* and J. Edwin Orr; University of British Columbia, 3 March 1950.
2. Flavius Josephus, *Antiquities,* 18:33; Suetonius Tranquillus, *The Life of Claudius,* 25:4; Plinius Secundus, *Epistles,* 10:96.
3. F. F. Bruce, *The New Testament Documents,* p. 119; cf. *Encyclopaedia Britannica.*
4. Cf. Frank Ballard, *The Miracles of Unbelief,* p. 251.
5. Frank Mead, *Encyclopedia of Religious Quotations,* pp. 49, 56 and 163.
6. John 10:30–33; 14:9.

7. Mark 14:62 and Matthew 26:64.
8. John 8:58.
9. Matthew 24:35.
10. John 1:1.
11. My Greek professor, Dr. J. R. Mantey, contradicted the Jehovah's Witnesses at this point, despite their citation of his writings.
12. John 20:28 and Hebrews 1:8.
13. Titus 2:13 (RSV).
14. Matthew 3:3, quoting Isaiah 40:3; John 12:41, quoting Isaiah 6:1; and Hebrews 1:6, quoting Psalm 97:7.
15. John 1:4; Hebrews 7:16; Hebrews 13:6.
16. See also John 8:58; 17:5; 1:1; and Revelation 21:6.
17. John 14:6; 1 John 3:16; John 6:69.
18. Matthew 28:20 and Revelation 1:8; John 2:24–25 and Colossians 2:3; Matthew 28:20 and Ephesians 1:23.
19. Colossians 1:16 and Hebrews 1:3.
20. John 5:23; Philippians 2:10 and Hebrews 13:21.
21. Matthew 1:18–25; Luke 1:26–39 and 2:1–14.
22. See *Pseudo-Barnabas in the Context of Muslim-Christian Apologetics*, Christian Study Center, Rawalpindi, 1974 (Dr. Jan Stomp), for background of Koranic error.

A Li

Abbott,
Anderso
  don
——.
  Pre
Ayer, A
Baillie,
  ver
Ballard,
Blum, F
  Un
Bruce, F
  ing
——.
  Gr
Burrill,
  tru
Carnell
  Ra
Clark,
  Pa
Compto
  sit
Coplest
Coulso
  Ur
Deane,
Dulles,
  Bc
Ferré,
  Y
Feuerb
  G

Filby, F. A. *Creation Revealed*. London: Paternoster, 1964.

Flew, Antony, and MacIntyre, A. *New Essays in Philosophical Theology*. New York: Macmillan, 1964.

Fuller, D. P. *Easter Faith and History*. Grand Rapids: Wm. Eerdmans, 1965.

Geisler, N. L. *Philosophy of Religion*. Grand Rapids: Zondervan, 1974.

Henry, Carl F. H. *Giving a Reason for Our Hope*. Natick, Mass.: W. A. Wilde, 1949.

Hick, John. *Arguments for the Existence of God*. New York: Herder & Herder, 1971.

————. *The Existence of God*. New York: Macmillan, 1964.

————. *Faith and Knowledge*. Ithaca: Cornell University Press, 1966.

————. *Faith and the Philosophers*. New York: St. Martin's Press, 1964.

————. *Philosophy of Religion*. Englewood Cliffs: Prentice-Hall, 1963.

Hope, Richard. *Metaphysics*. Ann Arbor: University of Michigan Press, 1960.

Hume, David. *Dialogues Concerning Natural Religion*. London, 1779.

Huxley, Julian. *Evolution in Action*. New York: Harper & Bros., 1946.

Jefferson, Thomas. *Life and Morals of Jesus of Nazareth*. Washington, 1904. (Compiled 1816.)

Jowett, Benjamin. *The Dialogues of Plato*. London, 1868.

Kenyon, F. G. *The Bible and Modern Scholarship*. London: John Murray, 1948.

Kuiper, G. P., and Middlehurst, B. M. *The Solar System*. 4 vols. Chicago: University of Chicago Press, 1953–1963.

Langdon, S. H. *Babylonian Epic of Creation*. London, 1923.

Lecomte du Noüy, P. *Human Destiny*. New York: Longmans Green, 1947.

Lewis, C. S. *Mere Christianity*. London: Geoffrey Bles, 1952.

————. *Miracles: A Preliminary Study*. London: Geoffrey Bles, 1947.

McDowell, Joshua. *Evidence That Demands a Verdict*. San Bernardino: Campus Crusade, 1972.

Marty, M. E. *Varieties of Unbelief*. Garden City: Doubleday, 1966.

Mead, Frank, ed. *Encyclopedia of Religious Quotations*. Westwood, N.J.: Fleming H. Revell, 1965.

Micklem, Nathaniel. *A Religion for Agnostics*. London: S.C.M. Press, 1965.

Mill, John Stuart. *Three Essays on Religion: Nature, Utility of Religion, and Theism*. London, 1874.

Miller, S. L., and Orgel, L. E. *The Origins of Life on Earth*. Englewood Cliffs: Prentice-Hall, 1973.

Neill, Stephen. *Christian Faith and Other Faiths*. London: Oxford University Press, 1970.

Orr, J. Edwin. *One Hundred Questions About God*. Glendale, California: Regal Books, 1966.

Owen, H. P. *The Christian Knowledge of God*. London: Athlone (University of London), 1969.

————— *The Moral Argument for Christian Theism*. London: Allen and Unwin, 1965.

Paley, William. *Natural Theology*. London: Faulder, 1802.

Pike, Nelson, ed. *God and Evil*. Englewood Cliffs: Prentice-Hall, 1964.

Pinnock, Clark H. *Set Forth Your Case*. Toronto: Craig Press, 1967.

Pollard, W. G. *Chance and Providence*. New York: Scribner's, 1958.

Ramm, Bernard L. *The God Who Makes a Difference*. Waco, Texas: Word Books, 1972.

—————. *Protestant Christian Evidences*. Chicago: Moody Press, 1957.

Rashdall, Hastings. *The Theory of Good and Evil*. London: Milford, 1924.

Reichenbach, B. R. *The Cosmological Argument*. Springfield, Illinois, 1972.

Reid, J. K. S. *Christian Apologetics*. Grand Rapids: Wm. Eerdmans, 1970.

Russell, Bertrand. *Why I Am Not a Christian*. London, 1927.

Schaeffer, F. A. *The God Who Is There*. Downer's Grove, Illinois: Inter-Varsity, 1968.

Schaff, Philip. *Companion to the Greek New Testament and the English Version*. New York: 1883.

Schonfield, H. J. *The Passover Plot*. New York: Bernard Geis, 1966.

Scriven, Michael. *Primary Philosophy*. New York: McGraw-Hill, 1966.

Stott, John R. W. *Your Mind Matters*. London: Inter-Varsity, 1973.

Tenney, M. C. *The Reality of the Resurrection*. Chicago: Moody Press, 1972.

Thompson, Samuel. *A Modern Philosophy of Religion*. Chicago: Henry Regnery, 1955.

Trueblood, D. E. *Philosophy of Religion*. New York: Harper & Row, 1957.

Weisz, Paul B. *Elements of Biology*. New York: McGraw-Hill, 1961.

Williams, Rheinallt N. *Faith, Facts, History, Science, and How They Fit Together*. Wheaton, Illinois: Tyndale Press, 1973.

Wiseman, P. J. *Creation Revealed in Six Days*. London: Marshall, Morgan & Scott, 1948.